adds value to business, work and life.

Employers are responsible for providing a safe and healthy workplace for their employees. OSHA's role is to promote the safety and health of America's working men and women by setting and enforcing standards; providing training, outreach and education; establishing partnerships; and encouraging continual improvement in workplace safety and health.

This publication provides a general overview of a particular standards-related topic. This publication does not alter or determine compliance responsibilities which are set forth in OSHA standards, and the *Occupational Safety and Health Act*. Moreover, because interpretations and enforcement policy may change over time, for additional guidance on OSHA compliance requirements, the reader should consult current administrative interpretations and decisions by the Occupational Safety and Health Review Commission and the courts.

This information will be made available to sensory impaired individuals upon request. Voice phone: (202) 693-1999; teletypewriter (TTY) number: 1-877-889-5627.

Edwin G. Foulke, Jr.
Assistant Secretary of Labor for
Occupational Safety and Health

Guidance for the Identification and Control of Safety and Health Hazards in Metal Scrap Recycling

Occupational Safety and Health Administration
U.S. Department of Labor

OSHA 3348-05
2008

Contents

OSHA®
www.osha.gov
**Occupational Safety and
Health Administration**

Introduction

The Audience for This Guide

Anyone who works in the metal scrap recycling industry—employers, employees, safety professionals, and industrial hygienists—should read this publication. This guide can help you identify and manage the hazards associated with exposure to various metals and processing chemicals and with related processes and equipment used in metal scrap recycling operations.

Why This Guide Is Important

Metal scrap recycling, also called secondary metal processing, is a large industry that processes, in the U.S. alone, 56 million tons of scrap iron and steel (including 10 million tons of scrap automobiles), 1.5 million tons of scrap copper, 2.5 million tons of scrap aluminum, 1.3 million tons of scrap lead, 300,000 tons of scrap zinc and 800,000 tons of scrap stainless steel, and smaller quantities of other metals, on a yearly basis. (ISRI NDa)

Scrap metals, in general, are divided into two basic categories: ferrous and nonferrous. Ferrous scrap is metal that contains iron, while nonferrous metals are metals that do not contain iron. These two basic categories of metals are described in further detail in the section, "Types of Metals Most Commonly Recycled" in the "Commonly Recycled Metals and Their Sources" chapter of this guide.

Many employees are employed by scrap metal recycling industries. Private, nonferrous recycling industries in the U.S. employed approximately 16,000 employees in 2001.[1] (Figures were not available for ferrous recycling industries.) In 2001, those nonferrous recycling industries reported approximately 3,000 injuries and illnesses. The most common causes of illness were poisoning (e.g., lead or cadmium poisoning), disorders associated with repeated trauma, skin diseases or disorders, and respiratory conditions due to inhalation of, or other contact with, toxic agents. Of those injuries and illnesses, 701 cases involved days away from work. The most common events or exposures leading to these cases were contact with an object or piece of equipment; overextension; and exposure to a harmful substance. The most common types of these in-

juries were sprains and strains; heat burns; and cuts, lacerations, and punctures. (BLS, 2003)

How This Guide Can Help

As an employer, this guide will help you protect your employees by helping you and your employees recognize, manage, and control the potential hazards associated with common metal scrap recycling processes. This guide will also assist safety professionals and industrial hygienists in their efforts to identify, evaluate, and develop appropriate controls for hazards related to metal scrap recycling processes.

What This Guide Covers

This document will assist employers and employees in recognizing and controlling typical health and safety hazards associated with various metal scrap recycling operations and in selecting appropriate control methods. This document does not provide an in-depth evaluation of every recycled material, or of every associated process-related hazard; rather it gives an overview of processes and related hazards common to a wide range of metal scrap recycling operations.

Employers must evaluate their own operations, processes, and equipment to ensure that all hazards in their operations are identified and appropriately controlled. There are many relevant guidance documents and standards related to exposure to hazardous substances (including metals), working in industrial environments, and working with specific types of material handling and processing equipment that may be associated with recycling processes. This guidance document includes references to these documents throughout the text, along with short summaries where appropriate.

Specific Standards and Requirements Addressing Chemical and Physical Hazards in Metal Recycling Operations

Although this guide recommends work practices and engineering controls to decrease hazards to employees, there are legal requirements in OSHA standards that you need to know about and comply with. These include, for example, OSHA General Industry Standards, *Title 29 of the Code of Federal Regulations (CFR), Part 1910* and the Construction Industry Standards in *29 CFR 1926*. Consult these standards directly to ensure full compliance with the provisions. States with OSHA-approved plans have standards which are at least as effective as, but may differ from, the Federal OSHA standards. These and

---

[1]After 2001, the data for private nonferrous recycling industries were no longer available due to a change in industry codes. However, the nonfatal injury incident rates in 2005 for codes that encompass the nonferrous recycling industry range from 7.8 to 11.2 per 100 employees (BLS, 2005).

other OSHA standards and documents are available online at www.osha.gov.

Other federal agencies, including the Department of Transportation (DOT), the Mine Safety and Health Administration (MSHA) within the Department of Labor, the Environmental Protection Agency (EPA), the Nuclear Regulatory Commission (NRC), and the Department of Energy (DOE) may each have applicable standards regulating specific types of scrap metals or specific aspects of related recycling processes. Employers should refer to these agencies for specific information regarding standards that may affect their recycling operations.

Other Relevant Guidelines
The American National Standards Institute (ANSI) publishes voluntary consensus standards on the safe care and use of specific machinery. ANSI standards also may give you guidance on complying with OSHA performance-based standards, such as 29 CFR 1910.212, *General Requirements for All Machines*. ANSI standards are sometimes incorporated into OSHA regulations, and in these cases, employers are accountable for complying with the specific versions of the ANSI standard referenced. OSHA generally recommends, however, that employers use the most recent versions of ANSI standards.

Types of Hazards in Metal Scrap Recycling
Employees in facilities that recycle metal scrap are exposed to a range of safety hazards associated with material handling methods, hazards associated with the metals themselves (as dust or fumes), and with the hazardous substances used to process or recover these metals. These hazards, the processes and operations that present the hazards and the related control measures are covered in this guide.

www.osha.gov
**Occupational Safety and
Health Administration**

Commonly Recycled Metals and Their Sources

Types of Metals Most Commonly Recycled

The scrap metal recycling industry encompasses a wide range of metals. Some of the most commonly-recycled metals (by volume) are iron and scrap steel (ISS), copper, aluminum, lead, zinc, and stainless steel. (ISRI NDa)

Scrap metals, in general, are divided into two basic categories: ferrous and nonferrous. Ferrous scrap is metal that contains iron. Iron and steel (which contains iron) can be processed and remelted repeatedly to form new objects. (ISRI NDb)

Common nonferrous metals are copper, brass, aluminum, zinc, magnesium, tin, nickel, and lead. Nonferrous metals also include precious and exotic metals. Precious metals are metals with a high market value in any form, such as gold, silver, and platinum. Exotic metals contain rare elements such as cobalt, mercury, titanium, tungsten, arsenic, beryllium, bismuth, cerium, cadmium, niobium, indium, gallium, germanium, lithium, selenium, tantalum, tellurium, vanadium, and zirconium.

Some types of metals are radioactive. These may be "naturally-occurring" or may be formed as by-products of nuclear reactions. Metals that have been exposed to radioactive sources may also become radioactive in settings such as medical environments, research laboratories, or nuclear power plants.

Common Sources of Recycled Metals

Ferrous scrap comes from sources such as:
* Mill scrap (from primary processing).
* Used construction beams, plates, pipes, tubes, wiring, and shot.
* Old automobiles and other automotive scraps.
* Boat scrap, railroad scrap, and railcar scrap.
* Miscellaneous scrap metal.

Ferrous metals are magnetic and are often collected in scrap yards by a large electromagnet attached to a crane, sweeping across piles of scrap to grab magnetic objects.

Aluminum is the most widely-recycled nonferrous metal. (ISRI NDc) The major sources of nonferrous scrap are industrial or new scrap, and obsolete scrap. Industrial or new scrap may include:
* Aluminum left over when can lids are punched out of sheets.
* Brass from lock manufacturing.
* Copper from tubing manufacturing.

Obsolete scrap, the other major source, may include:
* Copper cables.
* Copper household products.
* Copper and zinc pipes and radiators.
* Zinc from die-cast alloys in cars.
* Aluminum from used beverage cans.
* Aluminum from building siding.
* Platinum from automobile catalytic converters.
* Gold from electronic applications.
* Silver from used photographic film.
* Nickel from stainless steel.
* Lead from battery plates. (ISRI NDc; OECD 1995)

Nonferrous metals can also be recycled from captured particle emissions from metal primary or secondary production facilities.

Other exotic and precious metals come from a variety of sources, such as:
* Gallium from gallium arsenide (GaAs) used in electronics.
* Gold from precious metals manufacturing plants and from discarded electronics and jewelry.
* Platinum-group metals from catalysts (including catalytic converters, which automobile recyclers systematically collect).
* Used catalysts from industrial processes (mostly from the chemical and pharmaceutical industries).
* Old electronics equipment.
* Other jewelry. (USGS 2001)

Radioactive metal scrap may come from military applications (such as depleted uranium), discarded medical equipment, building or storage material from nuclear power plants (particularly nickel scrap) or trace amounts found elsewhere, such as Americium (Am-241), found in smoke detectors.

Additional information on sources of various metals is provided in the "What You Need to Know about Exposure to Other Metals" section at page 24.

What You Need to Know about Scrap Quality and Contaminants

The worldwide scrap metal recycling industry has developed sets of specifications and grading systems to ensure consistent quality of source scrap material for a given grade of metal scrap. The three most widely-used specifications are the Scrap Specifications Circular (U.S. Institute of Scrap Recycling Industries, Inc.), the European Classification for Non-Ferrous Scrap Metals, and the Standard Classification for Non-Ferrous Scrap Metals (U.S. National Association of Secondary Materials Industries, Inc.). These specifications generally set minimum and maximum content of certain metal impurities, and restrict levels of certain hazardous metals and other hazardous substances.

Employers should be aware that these criteria are designed to protect the end-user, or are for product quality purposes, and are not designed to protect employees performing metal scrap recycling processes. As a result, concentrations of certain metals that are below these quality specification requirements, either as incoming raw scrap or as processed scrap (to be sent elsewhere), may still pose hazards to employees handling metal scrap.

Employers should be aware of the potential impurities in their source scrap, and should be prepared to monitor for hazardous levels of those metals and other chemicals in their work environments (OECD 1995). Employers should also ensure that they receive their scrap supply from reliable sources that follow the established guidelines and should obtain material data safety sheets (MSDSs) and labels for the scrap materials where available. If an MSDS is not provided, the employer must request one from their supplier. See the discussion on "What You Need to Know about Hazard Communication" at page 32 in the "Recognizing and Controlling Hazards" section of this guide for more information on employer obligations to obtain MSDSs and labels for scrap materials.

www.osha.gov
Occupational Safety and
Health Administration

Common Recycling Processes, Hazards and Related Controls

Processes Commonly Used to Recycle Metal Scrap and Their Hazards

Metal scrap recycling is a large and complex industry. The variety of metals involved and the wide range of sources of metal scrap require many processing techniques. These processing techniques pose a range of safety and health hazards to employees in the industry. This section discusses a selection of those processes, the types of hazards that these processes may pose to employees, and control measures employers and operators can implement to control or eliminate these hazards. This document does not go into detail on every process or every hazard associated with every process, but rather it discusses the most common processes and provides examples of hazards related to those processes.

Recycling is a multi-step process, starting with collection and transport of raw scrap, pretreatment, melting, refining, forming and finishing. The recycling processes discussed in this document fall into these basic categories:

- Loading and unloading.
- Breaking and separating.
- Gas torch cutting.
- Non-gas torch cutting and other cutting.
- Baling, compacting, and shredding.
- Melting and baking in furnaces and ovens.
- Applying chemical processes to recycle metals.

Each category is an individual component of the recycling process and may pose a wide range of safety hazards that are common to many industrial and material handling processes. Such hazards may include flying pieces of material, exposed moving parts, fire hazards, and noise hazards.

Hazardous chemical exposures to employees are most likely to result from hot processes that produce fumes (such as torching and welding or melting in furnaces) or processes that produce dust (such as breaking, shredding, and cutting). Each of these processes is discussed in detail on the following pages.

Applicable Standards
29 CFR 1910 General Industry - many standards for occupational safety and health may apply to metal scrap recycling, including (but not limited to) the following standards
- 29 CFR 1910.1000, *Air Contaminants*
- 29 CFR 1910.212, *General requirements for all machines*
- 29 CFR 1910.219, *Mechanical power-transmission apparatus*
- 29 CFR 1910.147, *The control of hazardous energy (lockout/tagout)*

Sources of Additional Information
- OSHA 3170, *Safeguarding Equipment and Protecting Employees from Amputations*
- OSHA 2254, *Training Requirements in OSHA Standards and Training Guidelines*
- OSHA Health and Safety Topics: Machine Guarding, http://www.osha.gov/SLTC/machine guarding/index.html
- OSHA Lockout/Tagout eTool http://www. osha.gov/dts/osta/loto training/index.htm
- National Electrical Code 250-112

Loading and Unloading
The first step in any metal scrap recycling operation is getting the metal scrap to the recycling operation and collecting or sorting materials to be processed in groups. This may involve light or heavy trucks, stationary or mobile cranes, conveyor belts, and other large and potentially hazardous equipment. Working with this equipment poses hazards typical for material handling equipment.

Employers must ensure that employees use the appropriate combination of personal protective equipment (PPE) such as hard hats, sturdy boots, gloves, thick clothing, and respirators (if the operation generates hazardous dust) to be adequately protected from safety and health hazards.

OSHA's Personal Protective Equipment standards (29 CFR 1910 Subpart I) establish requirements for employers to evaluate the workplace and identify PPE needs based on actual workplace hazards (29 CFR 1910.132). These standards also establish criteria for proper selection and use of specific types of PPE such as foot, eye, or head protection. See the "Applicable Standards" box on the next page for a list of OSHA PPE standards (not necessarily all-inclusive) that may apply to recycling operations.

Forklift and crane operators must be properly trained in the use of such equipment. Operators must conduct pre- or post-shift vehicle inspections depending on vehicle use. Employers must consider equipping vehicles with guarding to protect any vulnerable brake lines from incidental damage during operation (NIOSH FACE; 29 CFR 1910.178). Of course, any alterations/additions to powered industrial trucks would require written approval from the manufacturer.

Case History #1
A 46-year-old laborer died from injuries sustained when his left arm became caught between the belt and pulley of a conveyor system at a Massachusetts scrapyard and recycling plant. The victim was working alone removing fallen debris from the conveyor frame at the time of the incident. (NIOSH FACE, 94MA021)

Preventive/corrective measures: Material handling equipment must be equipped with proper machine guards to prevent employees from coming in contact with moving parts. Emergency stop devices should be provided within easy reach of all conveyor operator stations to allow operators to immediately stop conveyors in the event of an emergency. Machines must be locked or tagged out during cleaning, servicing or maintenance. Employees must be properly trained in all safety devices.

Case History #2
A 41-year-old tow truck operator was run over by his tow truck while unloading a car at a scrapyard. The tow truck operator jerked the truck back and forth to release a car, and backed over the victim, who was working behind the truck. He then ran over him again as he moved forward, with the truck coming to rest with the victim pinned under the rear wheel. Scrapyard employees tried to rescue the victim by lifting the truck with a grapple crane but the grapple slipped and the truck fell back on him. (NIOSH FACE, 99NJ09101)

Preventive/corrective measures: Operators should disengage the transmission of the towing vehicle when hooking or unhooking vehicles from a tow. In addition, employees should never work behind the towed vehicle or between the vehicle and the tow truck during this process.

Case History #3
A 31-year-old male recycling plant foreman died when he was run over and crushed by a front-end loader. The victim was struck by the loader when its brakes failed as it backed down an incline after depositing cans into a hopper for processing. (NIOSH FACE, 95MA026)

Preventive/corrective measures: Operators must examine all powered material handling equipment at the beginning of each shift. All failing equipment must be tagged out of service and not used until repaired.

Case History #4
A 24-year-old forklift truck operator died after the lift truck he was operating overturned. The victim was operating the equipment in the storage yard of a wire mill. A length of wire became wrapped around the front drive trans-axle, severing the hydraulic brake line. As he was returning to the plant with two empty wire spools, the brakes failed on the truck. He was traveling down an incline and turned abruptly to avoid striking stored material. The sharp turn caused the truck to overturn. The victim tried to jump free but was struck by the Roll Over Protective Structure (ROPS) of the truck. (NIOSH FACE, 96MO054)

Preventive/corrective measures: Employers must keep aisles and passages used by material handling vehicles clear of obstructions. Operators must inspect all powered material handling equipment at the beginning of each shift. All failing equipment must be tagged out of service and not used until repaired. Operators of sit-down trucks need to be trained to remain in the operator's position in a tipover accident and to lean away from the direction of fall to minimize the potential for injury. When seat belts are installed on forklifts, employees are required to wear them.

Applicable Standards
- 29 CFR 1910.132, *General requirements*
- 29 CFR 1910.132(h), *Employer Payment for Personal Protective Equipment*
- 29 CFR 1910.133, *Eye and face protection*
- 29 CFR 1910.134, *Respiratory protection*

OSHA®
www.osha.gov
Occupational Safety and Health Administration

- 29 CFR 1910.135, *Head protection*
- 29 CFR 1910.136, *Occupational foot protection*
- 29 CFR 1910.137, *Electrical protective devices*
- 29 CFR 1910.138, *Hand protection*
- 29 CFR 1910.147, *The control of hazardous energy (lockout/tagout)*
- 29 CFR 1910.176, *Handling materials - general*
- 29 CFR 1910.178, *Powered industrial trucks*
- 29 CFR 1910.179, *Overhead and gantry cranes*
- 29 CFR 1910.180, *Crawler locomotive and truck cranes*
- 29 CFR 1910.181, *Derricks*
- 29 CFR 1910.184, *Slings*
- 29 CFR 1910.212, *General requirements for all machines*
- 29 CFR 1910.219, *Mechanical power-transmission apparatus*

Breaking and Separating Processes

Size-reduction of metal scrap is a necessary component of some operations. Basic metal breaking processes often involve heavy manual labor to break up large or complex assemblies of scrap metal, or to cut or break the pieces into sizes that can be fed into a furnace. Employees involved in activities of this type may be exposed to metal fumes, smoke, hot environments, and hot material when working near furnaces, and may come in contact with metals that present hazards through both skin contact and inhalation.

Some recycling industries use drop-ball breaking (or 'tupping') to break apart the largest solid pieces of scrap metal, or to initiate breaking up large assemblies. This process may create flying object hazards as the material breaks apart from the impact of the ball. Employers must ensure that employees are protected from these hazards by either performing the task remotely; placing a barrier or protective shield around the task; or using PPE such as face and body protection. Breaking may also create a noise hazard, requiring the employer to implement feasible engineering or administrative controls. If these controls do not sufficiently reduce the noise hazard, employers must provide appropriate hearing protection such as earplugs, canal plugs, earmuffs, or other protective devices as required by OSHA's Occupational Noise Exposure standard, 29 CFR 1910.95.

Sorting of scrap is now commonly done by automated processes, though some metals must still be sorted by hand. When sorting metal scrap by hand, employees must wear personal protective equipment such as gloves if there is a possibility of encountering any metal or other substance for which skin contact could result in adverse health effects.

Even for metals that do not irritate the skin, handling sharp or pointed pieces of scrap metal poses cut or abrasion hazards to hands or bodies. Employers are required to ensure that employees wear proper personal protective equipment such as gloves and durable clothing to guard against cuts and scrapes. Employees also need to be aware of the proper first aid, medical, and reporting procedures if they receive a cut or scrape. Similar concerns apply to other scenarios where employees work with scrap by hand.

Once an employee has started feeding material into a furnace, there is a risk of hazardous fumes from certain metals. Where exposures exceed OSHA Permissible Exposure Limits (PELs), employers are required to implement feasible engineering controls (e.g., furnace feeding operations can be set-up with local exhaust which can circulate and vent the air near the furnaces to remove toxic fumes from the workplace). If the exposures still exceed the PELs, employees will need to wear respiratory protection to prevent inhalation of toxic fumes and dusts. Refer to the section on Personal Protective Equipment in the "Recognizing and Controlling Hazards" section of this guide for further information on this topic.

Applicable Standards
- 29 CFR 1910.95, *Occupational Noise Exposure*
- 29 CFR 1910.132, *General requirements*
- 29 CFR 1910.133, *Eye and face protection*
- 29 CFR 1910.134, *Respiratory protection*
- 29 CFR 1910.135, *Head protection*
- 29 CFR 1910.136, *Occupational foot protection*
- 29 CFR 1910.137, *Electrical protective devices*
- 29 CFR 1910.138, *Hand protection*
- 29 CFR 1910.147, *The control of hazardous energy (lockout/tagout)*
- 29 CFR 1910.212, *General requirements for all machines*
- 29 CFR 1910.219, *Mechanical power-transmission apparatus*
- 29 CFR 1910.1000, *Air Contaminants*

Gas Torch Cutting

One of the most common tools used to break apart large metal pieces is the gas cutting torch, often used for cutting steel scrap. Classic cutting torches use gas, while other torches use plasma or powder, or even water (although water torches are rarely used for metal scrap). Thermal (gas) torches expose employees to sprays of sparks and metal dust particles, to high temperatures, to bright light that could damage eyes (light both inside and outside of the visible spectrum), and to various gases. Old cutting torches used pure hydrogen and oxygen, while newer torches often use acetylene, propane, carbide, gasoline-oxygen or other mixtures. (Nijkerk 2001)

Compressed gases may be flammable and/or explosive or may present toxic or asphyxiant hazards if leaks occur. Compressed gas cylinders can also present explosion or missile hazards if exposed to excessive heat or physical damage. OSHA standards at 29 CFR 1910, Subpart H establish general and selected substance-specific requirements for proper storage, handling, and use of compressed gasses. Additional requirements for compressed gasses used in certain types of welding and cutting operations are provided in 29 CFR 1910, Subpart Q.

The use of torches presents an obvious fire hazard. This hazard is of particular concern when working on materials that have combustible or explosive components such as motor vehicles with plastics and fuel tanks, or objects with wooden interiors (Nijkerk 2001). Disc-cutting is sometimes used to cut scrap metal objects, particularly where the heat and high temperatures of a gas torch would pose increased fire safety hazards.

Gas torches also involve storage of flammable and explosive gases on site. Employers must store these gases in safe locations and ensure that all equipment is in good working condition (i.e., detached or punctured hoses can create a safety hazard for nearby employees) (Nijkerk 2001). Employers must ensure that gas tanks are inspected, tested, and appropriately labeled while in storage and prior to movement and use. (NIOSH FACE; 29 CFR 1910.253)

Employers must ensure that employees use appropriate eye and face protection such as a welder's helmet and heatproof and or aluminum lined clothing to protect their bodies from the output of these cutting operations, which have similar hazards to welding.

OSHA has established PELs for many hazardous substances. OSHA requires employers to provide engineering controls or work practices to the extent feasible when employee exposure exceeds these PELs for any metal or other hazardous substances. Appropriate engineering controls such as ventilation may include a local exhaust hood or booth or portable local exhaust, such as a "snorkel" exhaust system. Where ventilation or other engineering solutions are not completely effective or are not feasible, employees must wear PPE (e.g., respiratory protection) to reduce their exposures to below the PEL.

Eye protection, such as safety goggles or a welder's mask with appropriate shaded lenses must also be worn by employees that perform welding or cutting activities (see 29 CFR 1910.133 for a list of appropriate shade numbers for welding and cutting tasks). Employers should ensure that a competent person inspects all work areas where hot work will be done and should also ensure that employees are capable of recognizing and avoiding hazardous situations. Note, a competent person is an individual who through training or experience is capable of recognizing hazards in the surroundings or working conditions and of identifying appropriate controls.

Case History #5
A 29-year-old scrap metal cutter died from injuries sustained in an explosion. At the time of the incident, the victim had been cutting a vehicle frame for salvage with a torch. He was working 8-to-10 feet from a 1,500-gallon storage tank. Escaping vapors from the tank were ignited by spatter from the cutting activities, causing the tank to explode. The victim was engulfed in flames, igniting his clothing and causing burns over 45% of his body. The coworker extinguished the victim's burning clothing and helped him walk to the company's shop building. (NIOSH FACE, 98AK021)

Preventive/corrective measures: A competent person should inspect all work areas where hot work will be performed prior to the start of the operations. All flammable and combustible materials should be removed from the area. If flammable or combustible materials cannot be removed from the area, employers must ensure that proper steps are taken to isolate the flammable or combustible material from the heat generated by the torch.

www.osha.gov
**Occupational Safety and
Health Administration**

Non-Gas Torch and Other Cutting

Materials that require higher temperatures to cut, such as pig iron and heat-resistant alloyed scrap, or materials that conduct heat too well to be cut with thermal torches, such as copper and bronze, may be cut with non-thermal methods such as plasma torches or powder cutting torches. These tools may also be used where a gas torch could pose a safety hazard, as discussed in the previous section. Plasma torches are often used for superconductors of heat or heat-resistant metals, such as alloy steels containing nickel and/or chromium (Nijkerk 2001). Plasma torches generate a large amount of smoke and noise, as well as ultraviolet (UV) and infrared (IR) light. Depending on the metal, this smoke could contain toxic fumes or dusts. A discussion on the potential chemical hazards and controls to reduce exposures to these hazards can be found in the "Recognizing and Controlling Hazards" chapter at page 16. However, where exposures exceed OSHA PELs, employers must install feasible engineering controls or work practices to reduce employee exposures such as providing well-ventilated areas for such operations. In addition, the employer should place appropriate barriers around the process to protect other nearby employees from exposure to the UV and IR light. Employees performing these tasks must use appropriate PPE such as respirators, goggles or face shields with appropriate shaded lenses, and hearing protection, to prevent exposure to smoke, fumes, light, and noise. See 29 CFR 1910.134 for OSHA's standard on Respiratory Protection, 29 CFR 1910.95 for OSHA's standard on Occupational Noise Exposure, and 29 CFR 1910.133 for OSHA's standard on Eye and Face Protection. Note, a list of appropriate lens shade numbers for welding and cutting tasks is also provided in 29 CFR 1910.133.

Employees using torches often spend long periods of time in awkward or hunched postures, which may increase the risk of bodily injuries such as strains and sprains. Other hazards common to cutting operations (as well as to welding and brazing) include burns, fires, explosions, electric shock, and heat stress. Even chemicals that are generally not flammable may burn readily when vaporized. Larger scrap metal objects are often broken apart using stationary shears, such as alligator shears used to cut apart short steel for foundries or to cut nonferrous metals. These machines can send small pieces of metal flying. Such flying object hazards may be controlled through the use of shields set up around the machines to protect employees. Eye protection and other body protection such as metal lined abrasion-resistant protective clothing may also be needed in some cases.

A larger concern than flying objects, however, is that the operator often works quite close to the machine and is subject to amputation or crushing hazards. In the early days of using shears, it was not uncommon for an employee to lose a finger or a hand to the shears, or to have a hand trapped between pieces of scrap that were fed into the shears. (Nijkerk 2001)

Hydraulic shears can be stopped instantly to prevent damage to the machine or operator, whereas mechanical shears transmit force from a flywheel to the shears and cannot be stopped quickly in an emergency. Hydraulic shears are, therefore, safer for the operator. Both types of shears, however, are still used in a variety of operations.

Modern alligator shears are often operated by a foot pedal that stops the shear immediately if released (Nijkerk 2001). Employers can also use controls such as wrist straps (attached to cables) to keep employees' limbs a safe distance from moving parts. One way to distance shears from the operator is to attach the shears to a crane. In this setup, the operator sits inside the cab of the crane and demolishes objects or cuts pieces of scrap metal from a safe location. If the metal scrap is being cut from a building or other object high off the ground, remote operation also eliminates the safety hazards associated with working at heights.

Hydraulic guillotine shears work similarly to alligator shears and pose similar hazards: employees must remain at a safe distance from the point of operation so that no limbs or other body parts could contact the cutting mechanism. Employers must install shields around stationary cutting areas to protect employees from flying objects.

When a tough or complex piece of scrap damages a machine, that machine may be more likely to malfunction and to pose a hazard to the operator and to other nearby employees. As a result, machines should have periodic inspections and should be maintained in proper working order. For all types of shears, employees must follow the company's established procedures for de-energizing energy sources and for lockout/tagout when performing servicing or maintenance tasks (see the OSHA Lockout/Tagout standard at 29 CFR 1910.147).

Case History #6
A 52-year-old welder was crushed to death by a hydraulic door on a scrap metal shredder. The victim was attempting to remove a jammed piece of metal from the hydraulic door when the incident occurred. Prior to removing the jam the victim did not lockout or de-energize the system. When the piece of metal was cut away, the hydraulic door, which was still under pressure, closed upward on the victim. (NIOSH FACE, 02CA004)

Preventive/corrective measures: Employees must follow lockout/tagout procedures to de-energize all equipment prior to cleaning or performing maintenance.

Applicable Standards
- 29 CFR 1910.147, *The control of hazardous energy (lockout/tagout)*
- 29 CFR 1910.212, *General requirements for all machines*
- 29 CFR 1910.218, *Forging*
- 29 CFR 1910.219, *Mechanical power-transmission apparatus*
- 29 CFR 1910.242, *Hand and portable powered tools and equipment (general)*
- 29 CFR 1910.243, *Guarding of portable powered tools*
- 29 CFR 1910.244, *Other portable tools and equipment*
- 29 CFR 1910.252, *General requirements (Welding, Cutting, and Brazing)*
- 29 CFR 1910.1000, *Air Contaminants*

Sources of Additional Information
- OSHA Safety and Health Topics: Welding, Cutting, and Brazing, http://www.osha.gov/SLTC/weldingcuttingbrazing/index.html
- OSHA Construction Safety and Health Outreach Program: Safety and Welding, http://www.osha.gov/doc/outreachtraining/htmlfiles/welding.html
- OSHA 3170, Safeguarding Equipment and Protecting Employees from Amputations

Baling, Compacting and Shredding
Scrap metal is often compacted using balers to promote efficient melting by allowing more metal into a furnace than would be possible for a random assortment of sheeting and other scrap objects. Balers use powerful hydraulic systems to compact scrap metal. Moving parts of balers must be shielded to prevent body parts from coming in contact with the machine. Car flatteners work on many of the same principles as balers and present similar hazards.

Balers are typically automated machines. This allows operators to stay a safe distance from the ma-

chinery, however, employees must still exercise caution when feeding raw material into a baler using a hopper or conveyor belt. Again, some sort of physical restraint such as railings may be appropriate to keep employees from falling onto these machines.

Some paper balers and shredders have sensors or heat detectors installed that react to human body heat and automatically stop all machine operations. For others, employees may wear magnetic or other devices on their belts that are linked to a safety interlock system (Nijkerk 2001). Systems such as these could be applied to some metal balers and shredders to provide additional protection to employees (both from metal and from contaminants in the scrap). Employees must be trained to understand the functioning and safety procedures of their equipment, and must follow procedures for adequate control of hazardous energy, particularly when performing maintenance procedures on equipment. (NIOSH FACE; 29 CFR 1910.147)

Case History #7

A 34-year-old laborer died after falling into an operating paper baler. The victim and a coworker were loading scrap paper into an automatically operated paper baler via a belt conveyor. The victim ascended to a platform located between the conveyor discharge and the feed chute of the paper baler to clear jammed material. Before ascending, the victim had asked the coworker to shut down the conveyor so that he could clear the jam. After shutting down the conveyor, the coworker turned away to get more paper. The victim fell into the baling chamber and the baler ram automatically activated. (NIOSH FACE, 9715)

Preventive/corrective measures: Employees must follow lockout/tagout procedures to de-energize all equipment prior to cleaning or performing maintenance. Employers must install guards on machinery to prevent any employees from contacting moving parts. Where access to process machinery is necessary, employers should consider installing standard railings using gates interlocked with the machine's control system. When the gates are opened, the machine will shut down.

For all equipment where pieces of scrap metal are fed into a machine directly, or using a hopper, or even via conveyor belt, employees must be trained in the proper use of the equipment. In addition, ap-

propriate guards must be installed to prevent employees from coming into contact with hazardous moving parts of the machinery. This applies to the alligator and guillotine shears discussed above, and also to other similar machines such as rotary shears and rotary shredders. For such equipment, employees need to stay a safe distance away from working machinery and take adequate safety precautions to minimize risks. Employers must install shields to block stray pieces of metal scraps from flying out from these machines and employees must be trained to know what materials can or cannot be fed into the machine to prevent malfunctioning.

In addition to the physical hazards associated with baling, compacting and shredding, these processes also produce significant amounts of dusts. These dusts, if not controlled, can present both explosion hazards and inhalation hazards. Some ways to control these hazards include:

- Installing proper air cleaning systems on shredding machines.
- Installing explosion sensors where appropriate to inject water to suppress explosions.
- Operating machinery at lower speeds to reduce dust generation.
- Introducing an inert gas to rotary shears to reduce the risk of explosion. (Nijkerk 2001)
- Providing supplemental ventilation where needed and perhaps respiratory protection to protect employees from exposure to hazardous dusts.
- Using wet or semi-wet shredding processes.

Some scrap materials such as scrap vehicles or refrigerators may contain fuels or other materials that introduce additional hazards to the process. Operators must be sure to remove these materials before introducing the scrap to process machinery. For example, gasoline must be removed from the gas tank of scrap automobiles before compacting or shredding the automobile. In addition, chloroflourocarbons (CFCs) and ammonia must be removed from air conditioning systems to prevent employee exposure to these irritants and to prevent the release of these gases to the atmosphere. Removal of CFCs also applies to shredding of refrigerators.

Many of the processes above use large amounts of electricity to operate. Employees must be aware of the hazards of working in high-voltage environments and should take appropriate precautions. All equipment power systems must be covered with non-conducting covers that require a tool to re-move. High-voltage areas must be protected to pre-vent access to unauthorized individuals. Employers must create a lockout/tagout program and train em-ployees on proper implementation of these proce-dures.

Melting and Baking in Furnaces and Ovens

Many scrap metal recycling operations heat scrap pieces to high temperatures to separate different metal components, increase the purity of scrap, bake out non-metal substances, burn off contami-nants, remove insulation from wire, or otherwise process the metal scrap (EPA 2001). This may be done using furnaces or ovens that use fuel or electri-cal heating sources.

Employees near operational furnaces are exposed to hazards even if they do not work directly with the furnace. Heating scrap will generate metal fumes if the furnace temperature is above the melting point of any of the metals in the furnace. In addition, hot pieces of metal could jump from the furnace, creating fire or burn hazards to nearby locations or people.

Similar to many of the processes already discussed, electrical furnaces use large amounts of electricity at high voltages to melt the metal scrap. Employees near these furnaces could face an electrocution haz-ard if they come into contact with a furnace in an unsafe manner. Employers must ensure that furnace refractories are kept in good condition and that em-ployees follow electrical safety guidelines. Employ-ers should ensure that there is sufficient room for employees to work safely in the vicinity of energized furnaces. For example, an employer may establish a maximum scrap metal size and weight for each type (and size) of furnace that they operate. (NIOSH FACE)

Furnaces generate smoke, dust, and metal fumes, depending on temperature and content. Combus-tion by-products may include sulfur and nitrogen oxides, and carbon monoxide and carbon dioxide. Organic compounds may be emitted as heating va-porizes oil and grease on scraps (EPA 2001). In addi-tion, heating or burning of certain plastics (such as plastic-coated wiring) may release phosgene or other hazardous substances. Emissions from fluxing typically include chlorides and fluorides. The highest concentrations of 'fugitive' emissions (i.e., gases and vapors that escape from equipment) occur when the lids and doors of a furnace are opened during charging, alloying, and other operations (EPA 2001). Employers should ensure that workplaces are well-ventilated, consider the use of local exhaust ventilation during these operations, and that emis-sions from furnaces are filtered before the air is re-leased outside the facility.

Afterburners can be used to control organic com-pounds, carbon monoxide, chlorides, fluorides, and hydrochloric acid; fabric filters can be used to con-trol metal oxide dust, chlorides, fluorides, and hy-drochloric acid; wet scrubbers can be used to control metal oxide dust, sulfur oxides and sulfuric acid mist; and electrostatic precipitators or fabric fil-ters can be used to control particulate or other mat-ter. These are used in different setups depending on the specific recycling industry. EPA (2001) discusses control methods for some recycling industries. For a full listing of hazardous air pollutants associated with some metal recycling processes, such as alu-minum production, lead smelting, iron foundries and steel foundries, see EPA's Emission Inventory Improvement Program (EIIP), Vol. II, Table 9.2-1. (EPA 2001)

For information on ventilation, refer to the "Exam-ples of Engineering and Work Practice Control Tech-niques to Reduce Emissions" section at page 29.

Case History #8
A 22-year-old male foundry laborer was electro-cuted when a piece of scrap metal he was loading into a damaged electric induction furnace became energized. The refractory had developed an un-usual degree of cracking, and molten metal seeped out of the refractory and solidified. This material was in contact with the frame, but not the coil. Two employees lowered the scrap into the furnace, which already contained molten steel. The victim was resting his thighs on the top edge of the frame. The furnace was jarred, and presumably more molten metal was released through the cracks, completing the circuit be-

tween the coil and the contents of the refractory. Current passed through the piece of scrap, the victim's body, and to ground through the frame. (NIOSH FACE, 89OH43)

Preventive/corrective measures: Employers should institute a regular inspection and maintenance program for all of their equipment. When problems with equipment arise, the equipment should be tagged and removed from service until it is repaired.

Applicable Standards
- 29 CFR 1910.147, *The control of hazardous energy (lockout/tagout)*
- 29 CFR 1910.212, *General requirements for all machines*
- 29 CFR 1910.219, *Mechanical power-transmission apparatus*
- 29 CFR 1910.1000, *Air Contaminants*
- 29 CFR 1910.1018, *Inorganic Arsenic*
- 29 CFR 1910.1025, *Lead*
- 29 CFR 1910.1026, *Hexavalent Chromium*
- 29 CFR 1910.1027, *Cadmium*

Sources of Additional Information
- OSHA Construction Safety and Health Outreach Program: Safety and Welding, http://www.osha.gov/doc/outreachtraining/htmlfiles/welding.html
- EPA (2001) Emission Inventory Improvement Program (EIIP), Vol. II, Table 9.2-1.

Applying Chemical Processes to Recycle Metals

Chemical processes are also used in a wide range of metal scrap recycling industries as a means to separate scrap into its component metals, to clean scrap metal prior to using physical processes, to remove contaminants (such as paint) from scrap material, or to extract selected metals from a batch of scrap containing many metal types. Chemical processes may include high-temperature chlorination, electrorefining, plating, leaching, chemical separation, dissolution, reduction, or galvanizing. Each of these processes may present specific safety and health hazards associated with how the process is carried out, as well as specific material hazards associated with:
- The starting reagents for the process.

- The resulting forms of these materials following any reaction.
- By-products.
- Special cleaning agents.
- The equipment used for the process.

As with every hazardous chemical introduced into the workplace, all employees who are potentially exposed must be trained in the hazards associated with that chemical category. This requirement and other provisions of OSHA's Hazard Communication standard (29 CFR 1910.1200) are discussed in the "What You Need to Know about Hazard Communication" section of the "Recognizing and Controlling Hazards" chapter of this guide.

The most probable emissions from these processes include metal fumes and vapors, organic vapors, and acid gases. Other potential hazards may include high amounts of heat, splashing of caustic or otherwise hazardous chemicals, or combustion hazards. Employers should be knowledgeable about the processes that are used in their recycling operations and should refer to MSDSs to obtain specific information regarding potential exposure to any other substances used in recycling processes. Employers must comply with OSHA PELs. They may also want to consider other recommended exposure limits (such as National Institute for Occupational Safety and Health (NIOSH) Recommended Exposure Limits (RELs)) for the chemicals used or produced in these processes.

One common process involves the use of aqua regia solution to remove gold from gold-plated objects. Aqua regia is a mixture of two corrosive acids. This process emits acid fumes that are dangerous to inhale. Employers using aqua regia or similar solutions (cyanide may also be used) must implement feasible engineering controls, such as a fume hood to remove fumes from the workspace. Employers must also ensure that employees wear gloves and an apron to prevent skin or eye contact with the aqua regia solution. Not all glove and apron materials protect from all corrosive substances, so employers need to pay special attention to the capabilities of the PPE used. For additional information on PPE, refer to the "Personal Protective Equipment" section in the "Recognizing and Controlling Hazards" chapter of this guide.

After smelting or separation, metal may be refined in an electrolytic process in which anodes from the smelting process are placed in an electrolytic cell that contains a cathode and an electrolyte such as sulfuric acid; the metal is deposited on the cathode. In such operations, employees must be aware not only of the hazards posed by the acid used as the electrolyte and the metal involved but also of the hazards posed by the electrical system.

> **Applicable Standards**
> - 29 CFR 1910.147, *The control of hazardous energy (lockout/tagout)*
> - 29 CFR 1910.212, *General requirements for all machines*
> - 29 CFR 1910.219, *Mechanical power-transmission apparatus*
> - 29 CFR 1910.1000, *Air Contaminants*
> - 29 CFR 1910.1200, *Hazard Communication*

Recognizing and Controlling Hazards

How to Determine the Hazard Levels of Various Processes

Metal scrap recycling operations present a wide variety of hazards, including health hazards associated with chemical exposures and safety hazards associated with material processing operations and the equipment used in these tasks. This section discusses the metals that may present hazards to employees in recycling operations, the exposure routes through which employees may be exposed to that metal and the potential health effects from that exposure. This section also addresses other chemical hazards of special note (e.g., metalworking fluids and radioactive material), and discusses ways that employers and employees can identify and control these hazards. Finally, the section discusses some ways that employers and employees can decrease the risks of employee exposure to these hazards. There is little data available to describe the level of air contaminants associated with specific metal scrap recycling operations. Employers and managers need to analyze the levels of various hazardous substances directly, using personal and area monitoring devices to assess employee exposures. After doing this, employers must comply with all OSHA standards. Employers may also want to consider recommendations by NIOSH (i.e., RELs) to determine the need for additional controls (e.g., engineering controls, PPE).

> **Sources of Additional Information**
> - OSHA Safety and Health Topics: Sampling and Analysis, http://www.osha.gov/SLTC/sampling analysis/index.html
> - EPA Emission Inventory Improvement Program, Volume II, Chapter 9: Preferred and Alternative Methods for Estimating Air Emissions from Secondary Metal Processing. (EPA 2001)

Metals that OSHA Regulates

OSHA regulates the workplace exposure to many toxic metals and their oxides. These metals are listed in 29 CFR 1910.1000 along with employee exposure limits and include the following:

Table 1. OSHA-Regulated Toxic Metals

Aluminum	Hafnium	Silver
Antimony	Iron	Tantalum
Arsenic	Lead	Tellurium
Barium	Magnesium	Thallium
Beryllium	Manganese	Tin
Bismuth	Mercury	Titanium
Boron	Molybdenum	Uranium
Cadmium	Nickel	Vanadium
Calcium	Osmium	Yttrium
Chromium	Platinum	Zinc
Cobalt	Rhodium	Zirconium
Copper	Selenium	

OSHA also has comprehensive substance-specific standards for hexavalent chromium (29 CFR 1910.1026), arsenic (29 CFR 1910.1018), cadmium (29 CFR 1910.1027), and lead (29 CFR 1910.1025). Each of these standards establishes workplace PELs as well as specific requirements for personal monitoring, medical surveillance, engineering controls, respiratory protection, and training.

Many of these metals do not pose any hazard to people who handle objects containing the metal in everyday use. In fact, low levels of many of these elements are needed for the human body to function. However, hazards exist when these metals are ground, blasted, roasted, or melted and fumes or metal dusts are produced and distributed in the air. Each of these metals may create health hazards to employees recycling scrap that contains even trace amounts of that metal.

Employers can typically determine the level at which a metal (or other hazardous chemical) poses a haz-

ard to employees by referring to the OSHA PELs listed in 29 CFR 1910, Subpart Z, Toxic and Hazardous Substances. Employers can obtain additional information on chemical hazards by referring to the NIOSH RELs listed in the NIOSH Pocket Guide to Chemical Hazards. Information on exposures associated with specific health effects of the OSHA-regulated toxic metals can be found in the references cited in this guidance document.

In cases where employees could be exposed to multiple hazardous metals or other hazardous substances at the same time or during the same workday, employers must consider the combined effects of the exposure in determining safe exposure levels. In such cases, employers must consult OSHA's standard, 29 CFR 1910.1000(d)(2), to determine how to apply exposure limits to exposure situations involving multiple hazardous substances.

Chemicals evaluated and found to be a suspected, anticipated, or known human carcinogen by authoritative scientific organizations, such as the National Toxicology Program (NTP) or the International Agency for Research on Cancer (IARC) may warrant special consideration at any level of exposure.

Employers must also rely on chemical manufacturers' data (such as MSDSs) when determining the hazards of workplace chemicals.

The remainder of this section discusses the health effects of selected commonly recycled metals that may be encountered during recycling operations. It also discusses where employees may encounter these metals. This discussion begins with a detailed description of six metals for which OSHA has provided comprehensive standards and/or guidance.

Applicable Standards
- 29 CFR 1910.19, *Special provisions for air contaminants*
- 29 CFR 1910.1000, *Air Contaminants*
- 29 CFR 1910.1018, *Inorganic Arsenic*
- 29 CFR 1910.1025, *Lead*
- 29 CFR 1910.1026, *Hexavalent Chromium*
- 29 CFR 1910.1027, *Cadmium*
- 29 CFR 1910.1200, *Hazard Communication*

Sources of Additional Information
- OSHA Safety and Health Topics: Toxic Metals, http://www.osha.gov/SLTC/metalsheavy

---

- OSHA Hazard Communication Web Page http://www.osha.gov/SLTC/hazardcommunications/index.html

---

What You Need to Know about Arsenic Exposure

The United States has not produced primary arsenic since 1985. All arsenic for domestic needs is imported, primarily from China (arsenic trioxide and arsenic metal) and Japan (arsenic metal). Historically, approximately 90% of the domestic use of arsenic was for chromated copper arsenate (CCA), a wood preservative that is now being phased out for residential uses due to concerns over toxicity. Some coal is rich in arsenic and arsenic is sometimes found in coal pollution. Arsenic compounds and arsenic metal are also used in electronics, pigments, and metal alloys, and are sometimes used in glassmaking. There is also limited demand for arsenic metal to be alloyed with lead and antimony for ammunition, solders, and other applications. (USGS 2001)

Arsenic may be found in contaminated workplace air resulting from smelting operations, in recycling facilities that deal with various nonferrous metal alloys, or with electronic semiconductors. Arsenic exposure can occur in the workplace through inhalation, ingestion, or dermal contact.

Exposure to high concentrations of arsenic can cause sore throats or irritated lungs. Breathing inorganic arsenic over long periods of time can cause damage to blood vessels and nerves in the hands and feet. Redness or swelling may result from skin contact with inorganic arsenic (ATSDR 2000a). Occupational studies have found increased risk of lung cancer among employees exposed to inorganic arsenic for many years. IARC and NTP classify inorganic arsenic as a known human carcinogen. (IARC 2006a; NTP 2004)

OSHA has a substance-specific standard regarding exposure to inorganic arsenic in general industry, 29 CFR 1910.1018. This standard sets a PEL of 10 $\mu g/m^3$ and outlines workplace requirements for the protection of employees from arsenic exposure including provisions for exposure monitoring, preferred methods for exposure control, written exposure control program, respiratory protection, protective work clothing and equipment, medical surveillance, and employee information and training.

What You Need to Know about Beryllium Exposure

Beryllium is used in alloy forms, as a metal, and as beryllium oxide. Beryllium is mined from two minerals, beryl and bertrandite. The United States is one of three countries that process beryllium ores. Most of the beryllium is sold to the domestic market, in sectors such as communications and computers, automotive electronics, industrial components, and optical media. (USGS 2001)

The most likely place for employees to encounter beryllium is the processing of alloy metals containing beryllium (http://www.osha.gov/SLTC/metalsheavy; http://www.osha.gov/SLTC/beryllium/index.html). Beryllium is often used as a metal in aerospace and defense applications, or as beryllium oxide in high-density electronics circuits (USGS 2001). Both of these sources may be recycled at some recycling plants. Beryllium is also used in copper and aluminum alloys and in sporting equipment such as golf clubs. Beryllium copper (a type of scrap metal that may contain high levels of beryllium) is processed by melting it in a furnace. Employees located near those furnaces may be exposed to beryllium fumes. Beryllium copper scrap is sometimes processed by other methods, such as chemical and electrolytic separation; thermal reduction and burning; melting and pyro-metallurgical separation; and milling (IPMI 2001). The melting process used for some other scrap metals may also generate fumes that can contain beryllium. (IPMI 2001)

Employees who breathe relatively low levels of beryllium dust and fumes may develop the lung ailment, chronic beryllium disease (CBD). CBD can develop over a few months or can take many years to develop. The disease occurs as a result of a person's immune system attacking beryllium present in the lung. These immune system cells attack the beryllium particles, leading to damage that can result in scar tissue in the lungs. This prevents the affected portion of the lung from functioning properly (Hathaway, Proctor, et al. 1991). There is no known cure for CBD (OSHA 1999b). Symptoms of CBD include persistent coughing, difficulty breathing upon physical exertion, fatigue, chest and joint pain, weight loss, and fevers. CBD only develops in employees sensitized to beryllium. A sensitized employee is an employee who has developed an allergic reaction to beryllium. Exposure to beryllium, possibly even below OSHA's PEL, may sensitize an employee to beryllium, placing that employee at elevated risk of CBD. (Bechtel 2001)

Many years ago, employees who breathed very high levels (>100 µg/m^3) of beryllium dust and fumes, even for a short period of time, developed acute beryllium disease (ABD). This disease rarely occurs in modern industry due to improved industrial protective measures designed to reduce exposure levels. ABD is caused directly by inflammation of the respiratory tract from irritation due to tissue exposure to beryllium itself. Symptoms associated with ABD include difficulty breathing, cough, and chest pain and occur much more rapidly than CBD symptoms. (Lang 1994) ABD may lead to death or respiratory illness similar to pneumonia.

Beryllium has been classified as a known human carcinogen by NTP and IARC (NTP 2004; IARC 2006a). Occupational studies reported excess lung cancer mortality among employees engaged in beryllium production and processing during the 1930s to 1960s. Exposure to large amounts of beryllium metal and beryllium compounds in the lungs of experimental animals has led to increased lung cancer. (ATSDR 2002)

As noted in the 1999 OSHA Hazard Information Bulletin, the current eight-hour time-weighted average (TWA) permissible exposure limit (PEL) of 2 µg/m^3 may not adequately prevent CBD among exposed employees (OSHA 1999c). Control of dusts or fumes is the main preventative measure. Industries that work with beryllium should consider their ventilation systems, employee PPE, and workplace monitoring for hazardous levels of beryllium. For additional control information, refer to the "How to Control Hazards" section of this guide.

Beryllium sensitization can be detected through the use of a blood test called the BeLPT, which stands

for beryllium lymphocyte proliferation test. This test measures how specific white blood cells called lymphocytes react to beryllium. A confirmed positive test result means that an employee is sensitized (OSHA I999c). While it is not known whether everyone who is sensitized will develop CBD, many exposed employees who were confirmed positive with the BeLPT already had CBD or were diagnosed with the disease at a later time.

All employees who could potentially be exposed to beryllium in the workplace should be taught to recognize the following symptoms as possible signs of CBD: unexplained cough; shortness of breath; fatigue; weight loss or loss of appetite; fevers; and/or skin rash. These employees should also be encouraged to talk to their doctor or other health professional about CBD and getting a BeLPT blood test regardless of symptoms. (OSHA 1999c)

Applicable Standards
• 29 CFR 1910.1000, *Air Contaminants*
• 29 CFR 1910.134, *Respiratory Protection*

Sources of Additional Information
• OSHA Safety and Health Topics: Toxic Metals: Beryllium http://www.osha.gov/SLTC/beryllium/index.html
• 10 CFR Part 850, Chronic Beryllium Disease Prevention Program, Final Rule. (Department of Energy, 9 Feb. 2006)
• OSHA. Preventing Adverse Health Effects from Exposure to Beryllium, http://www.osha.gov/dts/hib/hib_data/hib19990902.html.
• IARC 1997, Beryllium and beryllium compounds, http://www.inchem.org/documents/iarc/vol58/mono58-1.html
• EPA 1998, Beryllium and compounds, http://www.epa.gov/iris/subst/0012.htm

What You Need to Know about Cadmium Exposure

The worldwide production of cadmium was approximately 19,400 tons/year in 2005. In the U.S., only three companies produced cadmium in 2006: one produced cadmium as a by-product of the smelting and refining of zinc while the other produced cadmium from scrap, primarily nickel-cadmium (NiCd) batteries. (USGS 2007)

Cadmium is a toxic metal commonly found in smelting operations. Cadmium hazards exist for recycling employees cutting apart pieces of metal scrap with gas torches, and employees near furnaces that melt such alloys. Overexposure to cadmium may occur even in situations where only trace quantities of cadmium are found in the raw material or in smelter dust or fumes.

Nickel-cadmium (NiCad) batteries are one of the main sources of scrap cadmium (USGS 2003). Recycling of large NiCad batteries, usually weighing over 2 kg, typically involves emptying the electrolytes from the battery and dismantling the battery (cutting off the tops). The cadmium plates are detached, washed, dried and then sent to a recycling facility where the cadmium would be loaded into the furnace. Cadmium in smaller batteries is typically recovered by burning off the castings and separators in a furnace. Exposures to cadmium in NiCad recycling operations typically are associated with work near the recycling furnaces.

Historically, cadmium was also used as a pigment in industrial paints and may present a hazard to employees when welding, cutting, or shredding scrap coated with cadmium-containing paints.

Cadmium emits a characteristic brown fume (CdO) upon heating, which is relatively non-irritating. Several deaths from acute exposure occurred in welders who welded on cadmium-containing alloys or worked with silver solder.

Short-term exposure to high concentrations of airborne cadmium may lead to metal fume fever with flu-like symptoms such as weakness, fever, headache, chills, sweating and muscle pain. Acute pulmonary edema (excess fluid in the lungs) usually develops within 24 hours, reaching a maximum in three days: if death due to asphyxiation does not occur, then symptoms may resolve within a week (http://www.osha.gov/SLTC/metals heavy; http://www.osha.gov/SLTC/cadmium/index.html).

Longer-term exposure to lower levels of cadmium may cause lung or prostate cancer, kidney damage, and hypertension. Cadmium is also believed to cause pulmonary emphysema, bone disease, and possibly anemia, teeth discoloration and loss of smell (http://www.osha.gov/SLTC/metalsheavy; ATSDR, 1999a). Cadmium is classified as a known human carcinogen by IARC and NTP (IARC 2006a;

NTP 2004). Additional information is available in Cadmium, OSHA Publication 3136.

OSHA has a substance-specific standard regarding exposure to cadmium in general industry, 29 CFR 1910.1027, that establishes a PEL of 5 µg/m³. This standard also contains additional requirements for the protection of employees from cadmium exposure such as provisions for exposure monitoring, preferred methods for exposure control (including the use of separate engineering control limits (or SECALS) in selected operations), written exposure control plans, respiratory protection, protective work clothing and equipment, medical surveillance, and employee information and training. OSHA Publication 3136 provides additional details on these requirements.

Case History #9
A 36-year-old man was poisoned with cadmium fumes after smelting lead. Cadmium exposures can occur during lead processing since lead concentrates contain small amounts of cadmium which exist naturally in the environment. The patient developed pulmonary edema and died on the fifth day after exposure. (PIM 1990)

Preventive/corrective measures: All employers who use cadmium must monitor employees for exposure. In cases where employees are exposed above the PEL, employers must implement a full cadmium compliance program including provisions for engineering controls, warning signs, emergency plans, and PPE, among others.

Case History #10
An employee used an oxyacetylene torch to perform demolition work on a bridge which spanned a creek. He was assigned to salvage guardrails on the bridge and to also salvage a gauge shelter which was mounted on a platform next to the bridge. While wearing no respiratory protection, he spent the morning cutting anchor posts and bolts to remove the bridge rails; these were later found to be cadmium-coated. After lunch, he worked to remove the gauge shelter which was anchored to the platform on both an exterior and interior flange. Wearing no respirator, the employee entered the shelter and cut the bolts with the torch; these were galvanized. The employee felt ill after coming out of the shelter.

His condition continued to worsen; he was hospitalized two days later and died three weeks later. (OSHA IMIS)

Preventive/corrective measures: Employers are required to monitor employees' exposure to cadmium in all situations where employees may be exposed. If the monitoring indicates exposure to cadmium above the PEL, employers must implement a full cadmium compliance program including provisions for engineering controls, warning signs, emergency plans, and PPE, among others.

For additional details on control measures, refer to the "How to Control Hazards" section of this guide, at page 28 or to the OSHA website section on Toxic Metals.

Applicable Standards
- 29 CFR 1910.1027, *Cadmium*
- 29 CFR 1910.19, *Special provisions for air contaminants*

Sources of Additional Information
- OSHA 3136, Cadmium http://www.osha.gov/Publications/osha 3136.pdf
- OSHA Safety and Health Topics: Toxic Metals, http://www.osha.gov/SLTC/metalsheavy/index.html

What You Need to Know about Hexavalent Chromium Exposure
Chromium exists in several physical states; the most common states are chromium metal (Cr0), trivalent chromium (CrIII) and hexavalent chromium (CrVI). Chromium (in its various states) has a wide range of uses in metals, chemicals, and refractories. Chromium metal is principally used to produce stainless steel, alloy steels, and other nonferrous alloys to improve structural and anticorrosive properties. (USGS 2005)

Hexavalent chromium and trivalent chromium compounds are often used in electroplating of metals and plastic substrates to improve corrosion resistance. Chromates (CrVI) are also used as pigments in paints, plastics, dyes and inks to impart corrosion resistance, heat stability, color and other qualities. Other major industrial uses of hexavalent chromium

containing compounds are in catalysts, as a wood preservative, and as a chemical intermediate to produce chemicals for leather tanning. (OSHA 2006)

Employees in the metal recycling industry can be exposed to hexavalent chromium when chromium-containing materials are heated such as during melting or welding of chromium alloys such as stainless steel or a substrate with chromium protective coating.

The major illnesses associated with occupational exposure to hexavalent chromium are lung cancer, nasal septum ulcerations and perforations, asthma, skin ulcerations and allergic and irritant contact dermatitis (OSHA 2006). Hexavalent chromium is classified as a known human carcinogen by IARC and NTP. (IARC, 2006a; NTP 2004)

OSHA has a substance-specific standard regarding exposure to hexavalent chromium in general industry, 29 CFR 1910.1026, that establishes a PEL of 5 $\mu g/m^3$. The standard also includes provisions for employee protection such as preferred methods for exposure control, respiratory protection, protective work clothing and equipment, housekeeping, medical surveillance and communication of hazards.

Applicable Standards
• 29 CFR 1910.1026, *Hexavalent Chromium*

Sources of Additional Information
• OSHA Safety and Health Topics: Hexavalent Chromium http://www.osha.gov/SLTC/hexava lent chromium/index.html
• OSHA 3320, Small Entity Compliance Guide for the Hexavalent Chromium Standards http://www.osha.gov/Publications/OSHA_small_ entity_comp.pdf
• ATSDR Toxicology Frequently Asked Questions (ToxFAQs), http://www.atsdr.cdc.gov/toxfaq.html

---

What You Need to Know about Lead Exposure

The United States is the world's third-largest primary producer of lead. Eighty percent of the lead ore mined domestically comes from Missouri. In 1993, the lead industry employed 600 employees in primary smelting and 1,700 employees in secondary smelting and refining.

Lead is used primarily in batteries. Other uses include ammunition, sheathing on electrical cables,

and for corrosion resistance and color characteristics (as pigments) in paints.

Lead is the most recycled metal, when compared to percentage output (ISRI NDc) with the U.S. as the world's largest recycler of lead scrap. Most recycled lead comes from batteries where the primary process involves breaking and smelting used batteries. (EPA 1995)

The lead in used batteries is often in the form of lead oxide, which easily forms inhalable particles. When working with old batteries, employees should also be aware of the corrosive acid contaminated with lead (Washington 2002). Lead-acid batteries are processed by:
• Draining the acid.
• Dismantling the battery using hammer mill and grinding.
• Washing and tumbling.
• Treating individual components by desulfurization.
• Feeding this to a blast furnace or electric reduction furnace to recover raw lead. (USGS 1999)

OSHA has developed the Secondary Lead Smelter eTool (http://www.osha.gov/SLTC/etools/lead smelter) to describe ways to reduce lead exposure to employees in lead smelting plants, with sections that focus on Raw Materials Processing, Smelting, Refining and Casting, Environmental Controls, and Maintenance. Many of the discussions that this eTool provides on smelting and processing of lead should give insights into hazards that may be encountered by employees that deal with lead scrap recycling.

Secondary processing of lead battery scrap and other materials recycled with that scrap typically produce air emissions containing other hazards including sulfur dioxide and particulate matter containing lead and cadmium (EPA 1995). For further information on the potential hazards from exposure to cadmium, refer to the "What You Need to Know about Cadmium Exposure" section of this guide.

Recyclers may also encounter lead when working with scraps coated with paints containing lead (especially scraps originating from bridge dismantling and rehabilitation and shipyards). Lead dust can be created by grinding, cutting, drilling, sanding, scraping or blasting surfaces coated with lead paints. Lead fumes can be created by using heat guns or other heating techniques to remove paint from surfaces, or by using heated cutting tools to cut through painted metal. (NYSDOH 2001)

Lead is also recycled from solder, cable covering, building construction materials, and residues and drosses from smelter-refinery operations (USGS 2001). Employees may be exposed to lead during any of these processes.

Overexposure to lead is one of the most commonplace overexposures in industry. OSHA has established the reduction of lead exposure as a high strategic priority. Lead is a systemic poison and overexposure to lead can damage blood-forming, nervous, urinary, cardiovascular and reproductive systems and may cause cancer (ATSDR 1999b, Navas-Acien 2007). Lead accumulates in the body over time and remains in the blood for a month, in organs for several months, and in bones for years (NYSDOH 2001). Lead affects:
- the brain and nervous systems
- reproductive capabilities
- kidneys
- cardiovascular system
- the digestive system
- the ability to make blood

Inorganic lead is classified as a reasonably anticipated human carcinogen by NTP and as a probable human carcinogen by IARC. (NTP 2004; IARC 2006b)

Early signs of lead poisoning include:
- tiredness
- headache
- metallic taste in the mouth
- poor appetite

Later signs include aches or pains in the stomach, constipation, muscle and joint pains, and memory problems. (NYSDOH 2001)

Employees who may have been exposed to lead should talk to a doctor or other health professional. Your doctor may order a blood lead test which will measure the body's lead levels.

OSHA has a substance-specific standard regarding exposure to lead in general industry, 29 CFR 1910.1025. This standard establishes a PEL of 50 µg/m³ and includes additional employee protection provisions such as preferred methods of control, protective work clothing and equipment, housekeeping, hygiene facilities and practices, medical surveillance and employee training.

Lead poisoning is a topic of extreme concern in the medical community. Employees that encounter lead at work must take precautions so that they do not accidentally take lead dust into their homes through contaminated workplace shoes or clothes. For example, employees must not be allowed to leave the facility wearing the clothes that they wore during their work shift, which may be contaminated with lead dust.

> **Applicable Standards**
> - 29 CFR 1910.1025, *Lead*
> - 29 CFR 1910.19, *Special provisions for air contaminants*

> **Sources of Additional Information**
> - OSHA, Lead: Secondary Smelter eTool, http://www.osha.gov/SLTC/etools/leadsmelter/index.html
> - OSHA Safety and Health Topics: Toxic Metals, http://www.osha.gov/SLTC/metalsheavy/index.html

What You Need to Know about Mercury Exposure

The United States relies on recycled material and imports to meet its mercury needs; no U.S. mine has recovered mercury as its main product in over a decade. Some domestic companies recover mercury as a by-product of other metals. Several companies recover and refine mercury; the largest end uses for this mercury are the production of chlorine and of caustic soda. (USGS 2002)

Mercury is typically used in electrical applications such as thermometers and other gauges, valves, switches, batteries, and high-intensity discharge lights; it is used in amalgams for dentistry, in preservatives, in pigments, catalysts, and lubricating oils, and in heat transfer technology. The most common environments where exposure is likely to occur are during production and transportation of mercury, and mining and refining of gold and silver ores (http://www.osha.gov/SLTC/metalsheavy/index.html). Mercury and its compounds exist in three general forms; elemental (metallic) mercury, inorganic mercury, and organic mercury.

Mercury may be present in any industry that works with mercury or with materials that contain trace amounts of mercury. Recycling of mercury lamps is

one industry that is at risk for exposure to mercury. Emissions testing in 1999 showed that facilities that process steel scrap could be a large source of mercury emissions (Sastry et al. ND). Other sources include electronic devices such as rectifiers, switches, thermostats, relays; thermometers; dental amalgams; and catalysts used in the production of chlorine and caustic soda (USGS 2001). Employees may be exposed to mercury when smelting metals that contain trace levels of mercury, or when smelting involving processes that use mercury. Employees could also be exposed to mercury when collecting or otherwise processing gauges containing mercury.

Exposure to high levels of metallic, inorganic, or organic mercury can permanently damage the brain, kidneys, and developing fetus. Mercury's effects on brain functionality may result in changes in mood or personality (such as irritability or shyness), tremors, changes in vision or hearing, and memory problems. Short-term exposure to high levels of metallic mercury vapor may cause adverse effects including lung damage, nausea, vomiting, diarrhea, increases in blood pressure or heart rate, skin rashes, and eye irritation. (ATSDR 1999d)

In addition to the OSHA PEL for mercury (29 CFR 1910.1000, Table Z-2), OSHA has published guidelines in CPL 02-02-006, Inorganic Mercury and its Compounds, for protecting employees from occupational exposure to inorganic mercury. These guidelines provide suggestions for exposure monitoring, medical surveillance, training, PPE, housekeeping, and personal hygiene facilities and practices. (OSHA 1978, 1985)

Case History #11

A college chemistry professor spilled a few drops of dimethyl-mercury on the back of her gloved hand while the chemical was being transferred between containers. She promptly cleaned up and did not think any more about it. This was the only time the material was handled outside of a closed container.

The first symptoms did not occur until two months later, and they were ascribed to gastroenteritis. Neurological symptoms appeared after an additional two months, and she died five months later of organic mercury poisoning.

A lapse time between exposure and the appearance of symptoms is characteristic of alkyl mercury poisoning. The amount of the chemical that was absorbed into the professor's body was estimated to be less than one-tenth of a milliliter (approximately 300 mg), or the equivalent of a single small droplet.

Dimethyl-mercury is absorbed through the skin and is potentially lethal in small doses. Exposure appeared to have occurred through the employee's gloves. This death by organic mercury poisoning was directly attributable to use of the wrong type of glove material for the chemical involved. (OSHA IMIS)

Preventive/corrective measures: Employees must be trained in proper selection and use of PPE (in this case, the correct type of gloves) and must be required to use this PPE when handling hazardous substances. Employees that believe they have been exposed to any level of hazardous materials should report the suspected exposure to their employer and seek medical attention promptly.

Case History #12

An employee was told to clean up some mercury that had spilled out of a device. Three days later he went to an emergency room for neurological problems. After two more days, he was moved to another medical facility for further treatment. (OSHA IMIS)

Preventive/corrective measures: Employees must be trained in proper spill cleanup procedures, including proper selection and use of PPE when handling hazardous substances. If regular employees are unable to effectively and safely manage potential spills, the employer must either evacuate the area or have an emergency response plan in place to manage uncontrolled spills or other releases. Employees who believe that they have been exposed to hazardous substances should inform their employer and promptly seek medical attention.

Applicable Standards
- 29 CFR 1910.132, *Personal Protective Equipment, General Requirements*
- 29 CFR 1910.134, *Respiratory Protection*
- 29 CFR 1910.1000, *Air Contaminants*

What You Need to Know about Exposure to Other Metals

OSHA has published extensive information on arsenic, beryllium, cadmium, hexavalent chromium, lead, and mercury. In addition to these metals, employers should also limit employee exposure to all other hazardous metals handled or processed in metal scrap recycling operations. This section of the guide discusses additional metals for which OSHA and other agencies have collected health information. The section also notes some of the common processing techniques for those metals, where information was available.

The current PELs for each of the metals discussed in this section can be found in 29 CFR 1910.1000, Table Z-1 or Z-2. NIOSH has recommended exposure limits for a number of these metals. The NIOSH RELs can be found in the NIOSH Pocket Guide available online at http://www.cdc.gov/niosh/npg/default.html. These exposure limits are summarized in Appendix A of this guide.

Aluminum is one of the most commonly recycled metals and can be hazardous to employees in recycling operations. Scrap aluminum mostly comes from recycled used beverage cans (UBCs), which account for over half of the recycled aluminum supply. The other main source is diecasts, which are mostly from the automobile industry (USGS 2001). Employees who process aluminum scrap might be exposed to high levels of aluminum dust in workplace air during pre-processing steps that involve crushing and/or shredding and drying. Aluminum may cause respiratory problems, including coughing and possibly asthma from breathing dust, and it may also cause skeletal problems in those with poor kidney function. High levels of aluminum were found in people with Alzheimer's disease, but it is not known whether the aluminum is a cause of this disease. (ATSDR 1999c)

Antimony is derived primarily from the recycling of lead-acid batteries (USGS 2002). It may be found in the air near industries that process or release it, including smelters, coal-fired power plants, and refuse incinerators. Occupational overexposure to antimony has been reported to result in eye and respiratory tract irritation, chronic lung disease, and possibly cardiovascular and gastrointestinal effects. (ATSDR 1992a)

Cobalt exposure may be a problem for employees who make or use grinding or cutting tools, or that refine or process cobalt metals, or that use cobalt or produce cobalt alloys. Cobalt is typically processed in an electric arc furnace operating under reducing conditions to adjust cobalt's chemical composition, or by roasting of spent catalysts, chlorination or leach milling, or by other chemical processes (USGS 1999; Jones 1998). Most recycled cobalt comes from used catalysts from the petroleum and chemical industries, cemented carbides used in cutting and wear-resistant applications, rechargeable batteries, superalloys, magnetic- and wear-resistant alloys, and tool steel (USGS 2001). Occupational overexposure to cobalt can result in respiratory irritation, chronic lung inflammation and pulmonary fibrosis. Possible cardiac and neurological effects have also been reported. Skin contact can cause an allergic contact dermatitis (ATSDR 2004a). IARC has classified metallic cobalt containing tungsten carbide as probably carcinogenic to humans and other cobaolt compounds as possibly carcinogenic to humans. (IARC 2006c)

Copper may be present in dust in industries that grind or weld copper metal. Direct metal scrap (primarily alloy scrap) is the main source of copper scrap, with other copper scrap coming from copper smelters and refiners, brass mills, brass and bronze ingot makers, aluminum and steel alloy producers, foundries, and chemical plants (USGS 2001). Employees might breathe, or have skin contact with this dust. Occupational overexposure to copper dust can irritate the eyes, nose and lungs and possibly lead to gastrointestinal disturbance. (ATSDR 2004b)

Iron and steel are used in construction and industrial uses including vehicles, bridges, machinery, tools,

buildings, containers, highways, and appliances. The primary source of obsolete steel is automobiles (USGS 2001). Steel is often coated with aluminum, chromium, lead-tin alloy, tin, or zinc (refer to the sections on those metals for information on their hazards). Steel mills melt scrap in electric arc furnaces or basic oxygen furnaces, or in blast furnaces (USGS 1999). Iron oxide is a red-brown fume with a metallic taste that can affect the respiratory system and damage the lungs after breathing high concentrations over many years. (http://www.osha.gov/SLTC/metalsheavy). Exposure to iron pentacarbonyl is acutely toxic and can cause acute lung damage (http://www.osha.gov/dts/chemicalsampling/data/CH_247500.html), however, this form of iron may not be commonly encountered in recycling operations since it is used as a chemical intermediate or catalyst and, therefore, is not in the final products. (ISP, ND)

Manganese is ubiquitous throughout the various grades of steel (averaging 0.7% manganese), and can also be found as a component in certain aluminum alloys. The main material recycled for its manganese content is high-manganese (Hadfield) steel, otherwise manganese is mostly recycled incidentally when recycling steel and aluminum (USGS 2001). Manganese exposures can occur during operations at steel and aluminum recycling facilities which consist of segregating scrap by content and cutting up bulky pieces as well as the melt and refining processes (USGS 1999). Short-term exposure to high levels of manganese can result in respiratory tract irritation and inflammation of the lungs. Manganese exposure, at high levels over a longer period of time, can cause manganism, a set of Parkinson-like symptoms that include mental and emotional disturbances, difficulty walking, and slow and clumsy body movements. Long-term exposure to manganese at lower levels may cause deterioration of certain motor skills (such as holding hands steady or performing fast movements) and balance. (ATSDR 2000c)

Molybdenum is mostly recycled from catalysts. Molybdenum is also found in alloy iron and steel scrap, where it is recycled to produce steel products (USGS 2001). Employees can be exposed to molybdenum dust during the processing of scrap which involves cutting, cleaning, and baling, and possibly calcining, drying, leaching, precipitation, and separation. Roasting, crushing, and abrading may be used in preparation for melting (USGS 1999) (http://www.osha.gov/SLTC/metalsheavy).

Nickel may be present as fumes or as dust in industries that process nickel scrap. Nickel is used in stainless steel, copper-nickel alloys, aluminum alloys, and nickel-based alloy, and is used in electroplating and welding products. Employees may be exposed to nickel by breathing fumes, by ingesting dust, or via skin contact. Other sources include emission control dusts, swarf, grindings, mill waste, and waste from the stainless steel industry (USGS 2001). Skin exposure to nickel dust can cause an allergic contact dermatitis, often at the skin site where the contact occurred. Some occupational studies of employees exposed to nickel compounds have found increased risk of lung and nasal cancer among employees (ATSDR 2005a). Most nickel compounds are classified as known human carcinogens by IARC and NTP (IARC 2006a; NTP 2004). Employees who inhale large amounts of nickel may suffer from inflammation of the respiratory tract, chronic bronchitis or reduced lung function. (ATSDR 2005a)

Selenium may be present in the air at some metal processing facilities typically as elemental selenium or selenium dioxide. Selenium uses are: as a substitute for lead in plumbing when alloyed with bismuth and in electronics including rectifier and photoelectric applications (USGS 2001). Occupational overexposure to selenium may lead to eye, skin, respiratory tract irritation, bronchitis, and breathing difficulties. (ATSDR 2003)

Silver is used in solder, which may be found with many types of scrap metal. Silver is found in photographic plates and solutions, and in silver recovery cartridges (VADEQ 2001). Other large sources of scrap silver include jewelers' sweepings, catalysts, electronic scrap, and other metal materials (USGS 2001). Exposure to high levels of silver for a long period of time may result in argyria, which is a blue-gray discoloration of skin and other body tissue. Argyria is permanent but it does not have any known health effects. Lower levels of silver exposure can also cause silver deposition in areas of the body. A study found that 21% and 25% of silver reclamation employees exhibited conjunctival and corneal argyrosis, respectively, and that 74% of the subjects exhibited some degree of internal nasal-septal pigmentation. The route of exposure may have been direct absorption by the eyes. No association was observed between these depositions and decreased visual ability (ATSDR 1990). Exposure to high levels of silver can also cause breathing problems, lung and throat irritation, and stomach pain. In some people, skin contact with silver can cause allergic reactions such as rashes, swelling, and inflammation.

Tin is recycled from can-making facilities, brass and bronze plants, and soldering operations (USGS 2001). De-tinning involves removal of tin from new or old tinplate scrap by immersion in a heated sodium hydroxide solution, a batch process that reverses the tin electroplating process (USGS 1999). Employees could potentially have airborne exposures from fumes and dermal exposures from material handling. Inorganic tin compounds typically enter and leave the body rapidly and they do not usually cause harmful effects. Overexposure to organic tin compounds can cause respiratory, eye, and skin irritation and interfere with the normal operation of the nervous, endocrine, and reproductive systems. (ATSDR 2005b)

Vanadium may be present as a vapor or particulate in air at facilities that work with scrap metal containing vanadium. Vanadium is primarily an alloying element generally less than 1%; the main supply of vanadium scrap for recycling comes from used catalysts (USGS 2001). Overexposure to vanadium can cause harmful health effects to the respiratory tract (such as lung irritation, inflammation, and bronchitis), and can irritate the eyes (ATSDR 1992b). Vanadium pentoxide is classified as a possible human carcinogen by IARC. (IARC 2006c)

Zinc is found as dust or fumes in air at manufacturing sites, and at recycling sites. The chief sources of zinc scrap are brass, die casting scrap, flue dust, zinc sheet, galvanizing residues, and zinc die casts (USGS 2001). Zinc is processed by boiling secondary zinc alloys and then capturing the purified zinc in a distillation column, or by casting galvanized residues into slabs, melting the slabs in furnaces and then condensing the zinc fumes. A more recent process involves dissolving the zinc coating from scrap in a hot caustic solution and then recovering the zinc from the solution using an electrolyte process (USGS 1999). Some zinc is needed for proper body function, but high levels may be hazardous. Breathing large amounts of zinc can cause metal fume fever, which is thought to be an immune response that affects the lungs and body temperature. (ATSDR 2005c)

> **Applicable Standards**
> • 29 CFR 1910.1000, *Air Contaminants*

> **Sources of Additional Information**
> • OSHA Safety and Health Topics: Toxic Metals, http://www.osha.gov/SLTC/metalsheavy/index.html
> • ATSDR Toxicology Frequently Asked Questions (ToxFAQs), http://www.atsdr.cdc.gov/toxfaq.html

What You Need to Know about Radioactive Scrap

Scrap recycling industries may encounter radioactive metal scrap (Nijkerk 2001). This scrap could consist of scrap from decommissioned nuclear power plants (steel, galvanized iron, copper, Inconel, lead, bronze, aluminum, brass, nickel, precious metals), industrial and research irradiator activities, teletherapy, industrial radiography, medical equipment, gauges, logging, and pipes from the potash industry (Legare ND), or from other sources.

Radioactive materials may pose adverse health effects to employees, including cancer. Employees could be exposed to radioactive material or dust when contaminated materials are crushed or ground. If radioactive materials or objects are smelted, sealed sources of radioactivity may rupture and release their radioactive contents. Radioactive scrap in an uncontrolled setting in a processing facility may cause problems with the machinery, and require an extensive cleanup effort and possible temporary shutdown of the facility.

To detect radioactive material when it enters the recycling facility, employers can install a radiation monitoring system to detect gamma radiation emitting from source materials. These systems are expensive to purchase and expensive to calibrate and maintain. It is also possible to monitor incoming material with hand-held radiation detection devices which can monitor for alpha, beta, and gamma radiation, but these devices may be less sensitive and they require more operator skill. (Smith ND)

Fixed radiation-monitoring systems are generally installed at the loading area of a scrap facility, typically at the weigh bridge. Factors such as the type of radiation emitted, the distance from monitors, shielding, and background radiation may affect the ability of the monitoring systems to register all radioactivity. It may be necessary to install multiple fixed radiation-monitoring systems to monitor the same batch of scrap metal; common locations to install such sys-

tems are at the shredder or furnace entry, or at a conveyor or sorting station. (Legare ND)

Employers should work with their suppliers to ensure that no radioactive materials are delivered and should also install radiation detectors as appropriate. Working with radioactive materials can cause various types of cancer. There are no early warning signs for cancer. Exposure to large doses of radiation could also lead to acute radiation syndrome which includes nausea, vomiting, diarrhea, bleeding, coma, and even death. Employers must communicate the hazards of radioactive materials to employees and should set clear instructions on how to remove any radioactive materials that are discovered.

Applicable Standards
- 29 CFR 1910.1096, *Ionizing radiation*

What You Need to Know about Metalworking Fluids

Metalworking fluids (MWFs), or sometimes called machining fluids, are "fluids used during machining and grinding to prolong the life of the tool, carry away debris, and protect the surfaces of workpieces. These fluids reduce friction between the cutting tool and the work surface, reduce wear and galling, protect surface characteristics, reduce surface adhesion or welding and carry away generated heat." (NIOSH 98-116). Employees are unlikely to encounter MWF in conjunction with the scrap metal they process, however, they may encounter MWF in the course of using various heavy machinery (such as hydraulic shears) to cut apart pieces of scrap metal. MWFs may contain toxic substances; skin exposure to MWF in liquid forms, or breathing in vapors/mists from MWF, can cause dermatitis, acute and chronic respiratory disease, skin cancer and other cancers (OSHA 1999a). Precautions for working with MWF include ventilation, PPE, and training for relevant procedures. Similar precautions apply to solvents used for cleaning metal scrap prior to processing.

Applicable Standards
- 29 CFR 1910.1000, *Air Contaminants*

Sources of Additional Information
- OSHA Safety and Health Topics: Metalworking Fluids, http://www.osha.gov/SLTC/metalworking fluids/
- NIOSH 98-116, What You Need to Know About Occupational Exposure to Metalworking Fluids

What Other Hazards You Should Know About

In addition to the toxicological hazards discussed in the preceding sections, employees may face hazards from trace metals mixed into the scrap, or from materials and chemicals associated with the scrap such as gasoline in old cars, flammable and hazardous plastics surrounding cables, paint on used beverage cans, or from metalworking fluids used to process metals. Some metals are processed by oxidation/reduction or other chemical processes which may release harmful gases or harmful gaseous forms of the metal being processed.

The equipment used to process scrap metal may include physical processes that cut, slice, compact, shred, or perform other operations. These pose hazards to machine operators and those who work in close proximity to machine points of operation.

In addition, employers must also consider:
- Fire hazards from flammable metals or other substances.
- Explosion hazards from gas canisters, tanks, or cylinders, or from particles in the air.
- Injury from falling objects.
- Burns and scalding from hot air or hot materials.
- Other process-specific safety hazards such as amputation, acid burns, electrical hazards, confined spaces, etc.

Employers need to evaluate their metal scrap recycling operations to identify hazards present in their processes and to develop control measures. Employers should evaluate each piece of equipment to identify related hazards and to determine the best ways to control or eliminate hazards.

OSHA has guidance documents to assist you in considering many of these hazards.

Case History #13
An employee mixed sodium nitrate and aluminum out of sequence in a secondary lead smelter factory. As a result, the pot of lead exploded, burning and scalding 12 employees with molten lead. Five employees were hospitalized for more than one week. One employee died approximately 35 days after the accident as a result of the injuries he sustained. (OSHA IMIS)

Preventive/corrective measures: Employees should pay close attention to sequence when mixing certain groups of chemicals. Employers should provide written procedures for conducting hazardous processes. Where possible, these processes should be conducted in isolated areas of the facility.

Applicable Standards
- 29 CFR Subpart L, *Fire protection*
- 29 CFR 1910.106, *Flammable and combustible liquids*

How to Control Hazards

There are many ways to reduce the hazards the metal scrap recycling industry poses to employees. Engineering controls (for example, adding machine guards or barriers or installing ventilation, etc.) or work practice controls (such as establishing standard operating procedures or requiring the use of PPE) can place a safer distance between an employee and a potentially dangerous material or process. Employees must be protected (using engineering and work practice controls) from potentially harmful materials, and from the dust and fumes generated by these materials and the recycling processes. Workplaces should be well ventilated to remove dust and fumes from the air employees breathe. Employers must fully communicate the hazards of their operations to employees in such a way as to reduce those hazards.

Additionally, employers may need to conduct medical testing or medical surveillance to determine whether the exposure levels of certain metals and other substances have placed employees at risk. Medical surveillance is an important hazard prevention tool that can help employers detect and eliminate hazardous exposures that may be affecting employee health. Periodic medical testing is also important to help ensure prompt diagnosis and treatment of employees suffering adverse health affects related to exposures (http://www.osha.gov/SLTC/medicalsurveillance). Further information on medical screening and medical surveillance is available in OSHA 3162, Screening and Surveillance: A Guide to OSHA Standards.

The following sections outline some safety recommendations that are specific to certain operations, but many recommendations are common to a range of physical operations. Employers should become familiar with available resources on safety standards and safe work practices.

In all cases, employers must ensure that operators are fully trained to use their industrial equipment or vehicle and use caution during operation. Employers must ensure that defective equipment is removed from service until it has been repaired. Only trained employees should operate industrial equipment and vehicles.

Employers may need to design, develop and implement a comprehensive safety plan that includes, but is not limited to, analysis and control of vehicle- and machine-related hazards through use of a daily checklist. Equipment must be de-energized when employees are attempting to clean out fallen or jammed material. Employers must make sure that all electrically powered equipment complies with applicable electrical standards (29 CFR 1910 Subpart S).

Applicable Standards
- 29 CFR 1910 Subpart S *Electrical*
- 29 CFR 1910.1000 *Air Contaminants*

Sources of Additional Information
- OSHA 3162, Screening and Surveillance: A Guide to OSHA Standards
- OSHA 3170, Safeguarding Equipment and Protecting Employees from Amputations
- OSHA 2254, Training Requirements in OSHA Standards and Training Guidelines
- OSHA Safety and Health Topics: Machine Guarding, http://www.osha.gov/SLTC/machineguarding/index.html
- OSHA Lockout/Tagout eTool, http://www.osha.gov/dts/osta/lototraining/index.htm

Engineering Controls and Work Practice Controls

Engineering controls and work practice controls are the primary means by which an employer can attempt to reduce employee exposure to the hazards of toxic metal scraps and the equipment used to process those scraps.

Examples of engineering and work practice controls include:
- Enclosing processes where employees do not constantly need direct access to the machinery.
- Using product substitution to eliminate harmful substances.
- Installing an exhaust system to capture the airborne hazardous metal at the source.

- Installing guard devices at nip points where employees could come into contact with moving parts of machinery.
- Equipping all machinery with prominently-displayed and properly-functioning stop buttons, or a stop cable running the length of a conveyor belt or other equipment.
- Using explosion-proof electrical systems to reduce hazards associated with flammable materials or other combustibles.

Employers should also consider the use of alternate processes as a way to reduce hazards. For example, in some situations, employees can use other methods to cut scrap such as shears or power saws that may lower employee exposure to some toxic metals (e.g., hexavalent chromium) when compared to torch cutting. However, alternative methods such as saws and shears can still produce dust and noise and create certain safety hazards.

Work practice controls involve changing employee procedures and practices to reduce exposure to some substances. For example, employers may not allow employees to eat, drink, smoke, chew tobacco or gum in areas where hazardous chemicals are used or present. Both the lead and cadmium standards forbid eating or storage of food, consumption of tobacco products and application of cosmetics in regulated areas or areas where exposures have been measured above the PEL.

In addition to engineering and work practice controls, employers can implement administrative controls. For example, to reduce the number of employees at risk during a hazardous operation, an employer may consider performing the hazardous task during times when fewer individuals are present in the work area.

OSHA substance-specific standards for arsenic, cadmium, hexavalent chromium and lead contain provisions for change rooms and hygiene facilities such as showers and handwashing and luncheon facilities. Employers must also follow other requirements regarding clean surfaces; cleanup of spills and releases; and cleaning methods that minimize the risk of dispersing hazardous dust into the air. Refer to the specific OSHA standards for these metals for further information on these topics. Employers can also apply these controls for recycling operations that involve other metals to help minimize the possibility of spreading contamination beyond work areas.

Examples of Engineering and Work Practice Control Techniques to Reduce Emissions

Some common engineering control techniques to reduce emissions to the atmosphere include:
- Wet scrubbers for dust (particulate matter) and acid gases. Scrubbers work by passing the material through a liquid that absorbs the dust. Liquids are selected based on their ability to maximize pollutant removal.
- Thermal and catalytic incineration for organic compounds. Incineration uses burners and chambers to ignite fuel and to allow oxidation to occur.
- Cyclones, electrostatic precipitators (ESPs), and fabric filters, for filterable dust (EPA 2001). Cyclones work like centrifuges, spiraling incoming gases to cause heavier particulate matter to drop out of the air to a surface to be collected. Electrostatic precipitators use electrical static forces to collect particles out of a gas stream and onto collection plates. Fabric filters (baghouses) pass a gas stream through a porous fabric: the particles form a layer of dust that can be removed.

Other examples of common engineering controls:
- Adding machine guards or barriers.
- Local exhaust ventilation, which includes both portable ventilation systems and stationary hoods, is generally the preferred method to control emissions in the workplace. For example, cutters with local exhaust ventilation.

Employers should ensure that employees avoid prolonged skin contact with hazardous metals and other hazardous substances either through controlling fugitive emissions or providing appropriate PPE. In most cases, employers must not use compressed air to clean working surfaces or body parts. Ventilation is one of the main engineering controls used to control exposure to chemical hazards in the workplace. There are two basic types of ventilation systems used for this purpose: general exhaust ventilation which provides ventilation for an entire room or area and local exhaust ventilation which provides local exhaust at a specific work area or process.

General exhaust ventilation (i.e., dilution, ventilation) allows materials to be released into the general atmosphere of the workplace and then introduces uncontaminated air to reduce concentrations of dust or vapor to acceptable levels. General exhaust ventilation may be appropriate where:

- The contaminants released into the air constitute a low hazard.
- The contaminants are unlikely to settle.
- Emission is widely dispersed or uniform.

Local exhaust ventilation is designed to capture and remove hazardous dusts, vapors, or fumes at their source before they can enter the general work space. Local exhaust ventilation (such as chemical hoods) may be appropriate where the materials released pose a high hazard or are highly localized; where air does not already circulate adequately to eliminate the hazard; or where employees work in close proximity to the emission source.

Applicable Standards
- 29 CFR 1910.94, *Ventilation*
- 29 CFR 1910.1000, *Air Contaminants*
- 29 CFR 1910.1018, *Arsenic*
- 29 CFR 1910.1026, *Hexavalent Chromium*
- 29 CFR 1910.1025, *Lead*
- 29 CFR 1910.1027, *Cadmium*

Sources of Additional Information
- OSHA Safety and Health Topics: Ventilation, http://www.osha.gov/SLTC/ventilation/

Personal Protective Equipment

While engineering controls and work practice controls are the primary means of reducing exposure to hazardous chemicals and processes, they are not always completely effective. In such cases, PPE may be used to reduce employee exposure. OSHA requires the use of PPE to reduce employees' exposures to hazards when engineering and administrative controls are not feasible or effective in reducing these exposures to acceptable levels (29 CFR 1910, Subpart I). PPE may include respirators, coveralls or other full-body clothing, gloves, head coverings, boots, face shields, earplugs and vented goggles.

Employers are required to determine all exposures to hazards in their workplace, and to determine if PPE should be used to protect employees. Employers must provide PPE for their employees if the work environment or processes present a hazard or are likely to present a hazard to any part of an employee's body; or if an employee might come into contact with hazardous chemicals, radiation, or mechanical irritants; and potential exposure to these hazards cannot be eliminated through the use of engineering, work practice, or administrative controls.

A PPE program must identify and evaluate potential hazards in the workplace and indicate whether the use of PPE is an appropriate control measure. If PPE is required, the program must address selection, use, and maintenance procedures, as well as employee training and periodic reviews to evaluate its effectiveness in preventing employee injury or illness.

OSHA Publication 3151, *Personal Protective Equipment*, discusses PPE and the ways that employers and employees can identify hazards requiring PPE. For example, employees exposed to various safety hazards from operating heavy equipment may require adequate body protection including head and foot protection, gloves, durable clothing, hearing protection and safety glasses. Hazards from skin contact with materials can be addressed through the use of gloves and other protective clothing. A wide variety of chemical protective suits are available, and if such protection is needed employers must ensure that the suits used are appropriate for the materials of concern.

Some of the most significant hazards are associated with employee exposure to metal dust or fumes, so respiratory protection is a very important consideration. Respirators are required when exposures exceed the PEL and engineering and work practice controls are infeasible or insufficient. They may also be required in an emergency or in a designated regulated area.

Employers must provide respirators at no cost to employees, and ensure that respirators are used in compliance with applicable standards (29 CFR 1910.134). Respirators can be broken down into two general types, air purifying and supplied air. Air purifying respirators are typically tight fitting respirators that use replaceable filters to clean the air locally before the person breathes that air. They can have a facepiece that covers the whole face or one that just covers the mouth and nose. Supplied air respirators can be broken down into two categories, air-line respirators and self-contained breathing apparatus (SCBA). Air-line respirators connect the wearer's facepiece to a remote source of air either in a bottle or an air compressor. SCBA units supply air to users through an air tank worn on the user's back. Additional information on respirators is available in OSHA's Small Entity Compliance Guide for the Re-

vised Respiratory Protection Standard, Publication 9071, available online at http://www.osha. gov/Publications/SECG_ RPS/secg_rps.html or http://www.osha.gov/Publications/secgrev-current.pdf

Employees using metalworking fluids or chemical baths to dissolve or clean metal scrap may be at added risk of hazardous chemicals spraying onto their bodies or heads and would need appropriate protection. Employees that use high-temperature gas torches need eye protection for flying pieces of scrap and for different types and intensities of light and possibly full-body protection from the extreme heat generated by some gas torches. Employees who weld or torchcut stainless steel must be informed of the hazards of hexavalent chromium that is generated in the process and can be inhaled with the fumes.

Employers must dispose of and/or properly clean, launder, repair, and replace PPE. Employees should not be allowed to take work clothing or equipment home or off the work site, and are prohibited from doing so under OSHA's Cadmium standard, 29 CFR 1910.1027, and Hexavalent Chromium standard, 29 CFR 1910.1026. Employers subject to OSHA's Arsenic and Lead standards (29 CFR 1910.1018 and 1910.1025, respectively) must train their employees on the hazards related to exposure to contaminated clothing. Employers should provide clearly-marked containers for PPE and maintain separate storage areas for work clothes and street clothes. Further PPE suggestions are discussed along with each process, earlier in this document.

Applicable Standards
- 29 CFR 1910.132, *General requirements*
- 29 CFR 1910.133, *Eye and face protection*
- 29 CFR 1910.134, *Respiratory protection*
- 29 CFR 1910.135, *Head protection*
- 29 CFR 1910.136, *Occupational foot protection*
- 29 CFR 1910.137, *Electrical protective devices*
- 29 CFR 1910.138, *Hand protection*
- 29 CFR 1910.1018, *Arsenic*
- 29 CFR 1910.1025, *Lead*
- 29 CFR 1910.1026, *Hexavalent Chromium*
- 29 CFR 1910.1027, *Cadmium*

Sources of Additional Information
- OSHA Safety and Health Topics: Ventilation, http://www.osha.gov/SLTC/ventilation/

The Need to Provide Hearing Protection

Noise is a pervasive occupational health problem. According to NIOSH, 30 million employees are occupationally exposed to hazardous noise, and about one-third of these people have noise-induced hearing loss, nearly all caused by occupational exposure to hazardous noise levels. (NSC 2000)

OSHA requires employers to make hearing protectors and audiometric testing available to all employees exposed to 8-hour TWA noise levels of 85 dB or above. Employees must wear hearing protection if exposures to noise levels are 90 dB or above (8-hour TWA) or above 85 dB (8-hr. TWA) for employees who have experienced a standard threshold shift. These requirements are set to ensure that employees have access to protectors before they experience significant hearing loss. (29 CFR 1910.95)

Employees that work with or near heavy machinery including melting furnaces, or material handling equipment may need hearing protection for protection from noise hazards. The incidence of noise-induced hearing loss can be reduced, or often eliminated, through the successful application of engineering controls and hearing conservation programs. For example, employers can install sound-proofing to enclose loud processes or equipment to stop loud noises from traveling to all work areas. If engineering controls are not adequate to eliminate problematic workplace noise, employees can use hearing protection devices such as earplugs, canal caps, or earmuffs.

For additional information regarding OSHA requirements and guidance on hearing protection, refer to OSHA 3074, *Hearing Conservation*. To ensure compliance, employers should also refer directly to the OSHA standards in 29 CFR 1910.95.

Applicable Standards
- 29 CFR 1910.95, *Occupational Noise Exposure*

Sources of Additional Information
- OSHA 3074, Hearing Conservation
- OSHA Safety and Health Topics: Noise and Hearing Conservation, http://www.osha.gov/SLTC/noisehearing conservation/
- National Safety Council, Safeworker, http://www.nsc.org/pubs/sw.htm

What You Need to Know about Hazard Communication

Employees in the recycling industry may come in contact with a wide range of hazardous materials in their workplace. These materials may include the metals and scrap materials themselves as well as any chemicals used or produced in the recycling processes. Employers must ensure that employees are trained on the hazards of the metals and other substances that are in their recycling plants. In addition, employers must ensure that employees are trained on emergency procedures and that employees can obtain the required information immediately in the event of an emergency. Employees must be trained to wear appropriate PPE and to recognize situations where PPE is needed.

OSHA's Hazard Communication standard (HCS) (29 CFR 1910.1200) describes how employers are to identify and convey information about various workplace chemical hazards. The HCS requires chemical manufacturers and importers to evaluate the hazards of the chemicals they produce or import and provide information about these hazards and associated protective measures to downstream users through container labels and material safety data sheets (MSDSs). All employers with hazardous chemicals in their workplaces must develop and implement a written hazard communication program that includes provisions for container labeling, employee access to MSDSs and training for all potentially exposed employees.

Manufacturers and importers are required to provide information on the scrap metal they sell to recyclers. Manufacturers are also required to pass on any information they have regarding known contaminants of the scrap, as would be the case if cutting fluids were present. This information must, in turn, be given to the downstream users by the scrap recycler. However, the HCS does not require employers to create labels and MSDSs when they scrap manufactured articles, such as equipment, piping, radiators and furniture, when the employer scrapping the item did not manufacture it and does not, in fact, possess an MSDS for the item. Regardless, employers should check with their scrap supplier to determine if MSDSs and labels or other hazard information are available. If a scrap supplier obtains an MSDS from a manufacturer or distributor, the scrap supplier must make that MSDS available to any downstream user upon request.

The HCS provides employees the right to know the hazards and identities of the chemicals they are exposed to in the workplace. When employees have this information, they can effectively participate in their employers' programs and take steps to protect themselves.

Specifically, employees need to know about:
- The requirements of the HCS.
- Any operation in their work area where hazardous chemicals are present and the nature of the operations that could result in exposure to these substances.
- The physical and health hazards of chemicals in the work area.
- Work practices and other measures employees can take to protect themselves from potential hazards such as emergency procedures and personal protective equipment needed.
- The location and availability of the written hazard communication program.
- The content of applicable OSHA standards.

OSHA Publication 3111, Hazard Communication Guidelines for Compliance, and OSHA Publication 3084, Chemical Hazard Communication, discuss the requirements of the HCS in more detail. These documents discuss labeling, MSDS procedures, and other hazard communication requirements. Employers must consider special communication needs to ensure comprehension of the contents of the training program.

The substance-specific standards for Arsenic (29 CFR 1910.1018), Lead (29 CFR 1910.1025), Hexavalent Chromium (29 CFR 1910.1026), and Cadmium (29 CFR 1910.1027) also establish requirements (e.g., employee training, labeling, and posting of warning signs) for communicating the hazards associated with these metals to potentially exposed employees. Employers must refer to these standards for specific information on related hazard communication requirements.

Applicable Standards
- 29 CFR 1910.1200, *Hazard Communication*
- 29 CFR 1910.1018, *Arsenic*
- 29 CFR 1910.1025, *Lead*
- 29 CFR 1910.1026, *Hexavalent Chromium*
- 29 CFR 1910.1027, *Cadmium*

Sources of Additional Information
- OSHA 2254, Training Requirements in OSHA Standards and Training Guidelines
- OSHA 3084, Chemical Hazard Communication
- OSHA 3111, Hazard Communication Guidelines for Compliance
- OSHA Hazard Communication http://www.osha.gov/SLTC/hazard communications/index.html

References

American National Standards Institute (ANSI)
- ANSI Z87.1-2003, *Occupational and Educational Eye and Face Protection Devices*
- BSR Z89.1-1997, *Industrial Head Protection*
- ANSI Z9.1, *Open Surface Tanks Operation*
- ANSI Z9.2, *Fundamentals Covering the Design and Operation of Local Exhaust Systems*
- ANSI Z9.3, *Design, Construction, and Ventilation of Spray Finishing Operations*
- ANSI Z9.4, *Ventilation and Safe Practice of Abrasive Blasting Operations*
- ANSI Z9.5, *Laboratory Ventilation*

Agency for Toxic Substances and Disease Registry (ATSDR)
- ATSDR. 1990. *Toxicological Profile for Silver.*
- ATSDR. 1992a. *Toxicological Profile for Antimony.*
- ATSDR. 1992b. *Toxicological Profile for Vanadium.*
- ATSDR. 1999a. *Toxicological Profile for Cadmium.*
- ATSDR. 1999b. *Toxicological Profile for Lead. (Update).*
- ATSDR. 1999c. *Toxicological Profile for Aluminum. (Update).*
- ATSDR. 1999d. *Toxicological Profile for Mercury. (Update).*
- ATSDR. 2000a. *Toxicological Profile for Arsenic (Update).*
- ATSDR. 2000b. *Toxicological Profile for Chromium (Update).*
- ATSDR. 2000c. *Toxicological Profile for Manganese.*
- ATSDR. 2002. *Toxicological Profile for Beryllium. (Update).*
- ATSDR. 2003. *Toxicological Profile for Selenium. (Update).*
- ATSDR. 2004a. *Toxicological Profile for Cobalt. (Update).*
- ATSDR. 2004b. *Toxicological Profile for Copper. (Update).*
- ATSDR. 2005a. *Toxicological Profile for Nickel. (Update).*
- ATSDR. 2005b. *Toxicological Profile for Tin.*
- ATSDR. 2005c. *Toxicological Profile for Zinc. (Update).*
- ATSDR. ND *Toxicology Frequently Asked Questions (ToxFAQs),* http://www.atsdr.cdc. gov/tox-faq.html

National Institute for Occupational Safety and Health (NIOSH)
- NIOSH. FACE. NIOSH Fatality Assessment and Control Evaluation (FACE) Program. Online database. http://www.cdc.gov/ niosh/face
- NIOSH 98-116. What You Need to Know About Occupational Exposure to Metalworking Fluids.
- NIOSH, 2005 NIOSH Pocket Guide to Chemical Hazards.

Occupational Safety and Health Administration (OSHA) Standards
- 29 CFR 1910.19 – *Special provisions for air contaminants*
- 29 CFR 1910.94 – *Ventilation*
- 29 CFR 1910.95 – *Occupational Noise Exposure*
- 29 CFR 1910.106 – *Flammable and combustible liquids*
- 29 CFR 1910.119 – *Process safety management of highly hazardous chemicals*
- 29 CFR 1910.132 – *General requirements*
- 29 CFR 1910.133 – *Eye and face protection*
- 29 CFR 1910.134 – *Respiratory protection*
- 29 CFR 1910.135 – *Head protection*
- 29 CFR 1910.136 – *Occupational foot protection*
- 29 CFR 1910.137 – *Electrical protective devices*
- 29 CFR 1910.138 – *Hand protection*
- 29 CFR 1910.147 – *The control of hazardous energy (lockout/tagout)*
- 29 CFR 1910.176 – *Handling materials – general.*
- 29 CFR 1910.178 – *Powered industrial trucks*
- 29 CFR 1910.179 – *Overhead and gantry cranes*
- 29 CFR 1910.180 – *Crawler locomotive and truck cranes*
- 29 CFR 1910.181 – *Derricks*
- 29 CFR 1910.184 – *Slings*
- 29 CFR 1910.212 – *General requirements for all machines*
- 29 CFR 1910.219 – *Mechanical power-transmission apparatus.*
- 29 CFR 1910.242 – *Hand and portable powered tools and equipment (general)*
- 29 CFR 1910.243 – *Guarding of portable powered tools*
- 29 CFR 1910.244 – *Other portable tools and equipment*
- 29 CFR 1910.252 – *General requirements (Welding, Cutting, and Brazing)*
- 29 CFR 1910.253 – *Oxygen-fuel gas welding and cutting*
- 29 CFR 1910.1000 – *Air Contaminants*
- 29 CFR 1910.1000, Table Z-1 – *Limits for Air Contaminants*

- 29 CFR 1910.1000, Table Z-2
- 29 CFR 1910.1018 – *Arsenic*
- 29 CFR 1910.1025 – *Lead*
- 29 CFR 1910.1026 – *Hexavalent Chromium*
- 29 CFR 1910.1027 – *Cadmium*
- 29 CFR 1910.1096 – *Ionizing radiation*
- 29 CFR 1910.1200 – *Hazard Communication*
- 29 CFR 1910 Subpart H – *Hazardous Materials*
- 29 CFR 1910 Subpart I – *Personal Protective Equipment*
- 29 CFR 1910 Subpart L – *Fire protection*
- 29 CFR 1910 Subpart Q – *Welding, Cutting and Brazing*
- 29 CFR 1910 Subpart S – *Electrical*
- 29 CFR 1926.62 – *Lead in Construction*
- 29 CFR 1926.55 – App. A, *Gases, fumes, vapors, dusts, and musts*

Occupational Safety and Health Administration (OSHA) Databases and Web Pages
- OSHA IMIS. OSHA Form 170 Reports, *Integrated Management Information System (IMIS)*.
- OSHA eTool. OSHA, Lead Secondary Smelter eTool, http://www.osha.gov/ SLTC/etools/leadsmelter/
- OSHA eTool. Lockout/Tagout eTool http://www.osha.gov/dts/osta/lototrain ing/index.htm
- OSHA Safety and Health Topics: Main Page http://www.osha.gov/SLTC/index.html
- OSHA Construction Safety and Health Outreach Program: Safety and Welding, http://www.osha.gov/doc/outreachtrain ing/htmlfiles/welding.html
- OSHA Hazard Communication Web Page: Foundation of Workplace Chemical Safety Programs, http://www.osha.gov/SLTC/hazardcommunica-tions/index.html

Occupational Safety and Health Administration (OSHA) Publications
- OSHA 1620, Occupational Exposure to Beryllium (not yet released)
- OSHA 2254, Training Requirements in OSHA Standards and Training Guidelines
- OSHA 3074, Hearing Conservation
- OSHA 3084, Chemical Hazard Communication
- OSHA 3111, Hazard Communication Guidelines for Compliance
- OSHA 3136, Cadmium
- OSHA 3139, Occupational Exposure to Cadmium in the Construction Industry
- OSHA 3151, Personal Protective Equipment
- OSHA 3162, Screening and Surveillance: A Guide to OSHA Standards
- OSHA 3170, Safeguarding Equipment and Protecting Employees from Amputations
- OSHA 3320, Small Entity Compliance Guide for the Hexavalent Chromium Standards

Occupational Safety and Health Administration (OSHA) Releases
- OSHA. 1999a. Summary of Final Report of the OSHA Metalworking Fluids Standards Advisory Committee. July 1999. http://www.osha.gov/dhs/reports/metalwork ing/MWFSAC-FinalReportSummary.html
- OSHA. 1999b. OSHA Alerts Workers to Beryllium Exposure, Trade News Release, 9/17/99. http://www.osha.gov/pls/oshaweb. show_document?p_table=New_Release& p-id=283
- OSHA. 1999c. Preventing Adverse Health Effects from Exposure to Beryllium. http://www.osha.gov/dts/hib/hib_data/ hib19990902.html
- OSHA 2001. OSHA Launches National Emphasis Program to Reduce Lead Exposure, OSHA Trade News Release, July 20, 2001.
- OSHA. 1978. Directive 02-02-006 Inorganic Mercury and its Compounds.
- OSHA. 1985. Directive 02-02-006 CH-1 Removal of Obsolete Sections

Other References
ACGIH. 2004. Industrial Ventilation: A Manual of Recommended Practice, 25th Edition. 2004.

Bechtel. 2001. Hanford Site Contractor Chronic Beryllium Disease Prevention Program, Bechtel Hanford, Inc., Hanford Environmental Health Foundation, Fluor Hanford, Pacific Northwest National Laboratory, CH2M Hill Hanford Group, Inc. Rev. 2, April 26, 2001.

BLS. 2003. Occupational Injuries and Illnesses in the United States, Profiles Data 1992-2001, Version 9.0. Bureau of Labor Statistics. Department of Labor.

DOE. 2006. 10 CFR part 850, Chronic Beryllium Disease Program, Final Rule (Department of Energy, 9 Feb. 2006).

EPA. 1995. EPA Office of Compliance Sector Notebook Project. Profile of the Nonferrous Metals Industry. Sept. 1995. http://www.epa.gov/Compliance/resources/publica tions/assistance/sectors/notebooks/nfmetlsn.pdf

EPA. 1998. Beryllium and Beryllium Compounds. http://www.epa.gov/IRIS/subst/0012.htm

EPA. 2001. Emission Inventory Improvement Program. U.S. Environmental Protection Program. 2001. http://www.epa.gov/ttn/chief/eiip/

Hathaway GJ, Proctor NH, Hughes JP, and Fischman ML [1991]. Proctor and Hughes' chemical hazards of the workplace. 3rd edition. New York, NY: Van Nostrand Reinhold.

IARC 1997. IARC Monographs on the Evaluation of Carcinogenic Risks to Humans. Volume 58, Beryllium, Cadmium, Mercury, and Exposures in the Glass Manufacturing Industry.

IARC 2006a. List of Agents Evaluated and Their Classifications as Evaluated in IARC Monographs Volumes 1-85. http://monographs.iarc.fr/ENG/Classification/index.php

IARC 2006b. IARC Monographs on the Evaluation of Carcinogenic Risks to Humans. Volume 87, Inorganic and Organic Lead Compounds.

IARC 2006c. IARC Monographs on the Evaluation of Carcinogenic Risks to Humans. Volume 86, Cobalt in Hard Metals and Cobalt Sulfate, Gallium Arsenide, Indium Phosphide, and Vanadium Pentoxide.

IPCS. 2000. International Chemical Safety Card, Beryllium. NIOSH, CEC, and IPCS. http://www.cdc.gov/niosh/ipcsneng/neng 0226.html.

IPMI. 2001. Environmental and Regulatory Affairs Committee. Guidance to Members on Beryllium Management. International Precious Metals Institute. October 15, 2001.

ISP ND International Specialty Products Industrial Reference Guide Performance-Enhancing Products for Industrial Markets. No date. Online at: http://www.ispcorp.com/products/biocides/content/brochure/ind_ref.html

ISRI. NDa. Scrap Recycling: Where Tomorrow Begins. Institute of Scrap Recycling Industries (ISRI). No date. Online at http://www.isri.org/isridown loads/scrap2.pdf.

ISRI. NDb. Recycling Scrap Iron and Steel. No date. Online at http://www.isri.org/isri downloads/ironq.pdf.

ISRI. NDc. Recycling Nonferrous Scrap Metals. No date. Online at http://www.isri.org/isri-downloads/nonferq.pdf.

Jones, R.T., 1998 Using a Direct-Current Arc Furnace to Recover Cobalt from Slags. JOM, 57 1998 October.

Lang, 1994. Beryllium: a chronic problem. Leslie Lang. Environmental Health Perspectives, 102(6-7), June-July 1994.

Legare, J-M, PhD, ND. Detection of Radioactive Sources in Scrap Metal. Commercial Radiation Protection Services. No date. Online at http://www.sftext.com/radioprotection/ cuba_detection_radio.html.

Navas-Acien, A., Guallar, E., Silbergeld, E.K., and Rothenberg, S.J. 2007. Lead Exposure and Cardiovascular Disease – a Systematic Review. Environmental Health Perspectives, 115(3), March 2007.

Nijkerk, A.A. and Dalmijn, W.L. 2001. Handbook of Recycling Techniques. The Hague: Nijkerk Consultancy. Fifth, revised and expanded edition, February 2001.

NSC. ND. Accident Prevention Manual for Industrial Operations: Engineering and Technology. 10th Ed. Itasca, IL: National Safety Council. No date.

NSC. 2000. National Safety Council Safeworker program. February 2000. http://www.nsc.org/pubs/sw.htm.

NTP. 2004. Eleventh Report on Carcinogens, National Toxicology Program.

NYSDOH. 2001. Lead on the Job: A Guide for Workers, New York State Department of Health, January 2001. http://www.health.state.ny.us/nysdoh/lead/worker.htm.

OECD. 1995. Recycling of Copper, Lead, and Zinc-Bearing Wastes. Environmental Monographs No. 109. Organization for Economic Cooperation and Development (OECD), Paris, 1995. http://www.cpplatform.ch/technology/pdf_docs/1114b.pdf.

OSHA. 2006. Final Economic and Regulatory Flexibility Analysis for OSHA's Final Standard for Occupational Exposure to Hexavalent Chromium. http://dockets.osha.gov/search/browseExhibits.asp

PIM. 1990. Cadmium. PIM 089. http://www.inchem.org/documents/pims/ chemical/cadmium.htm.

Smith, DM. Radioactive Material in Scrap Metal - The UK Approach. Health & Safety Executive, Midlands Region Specialist Group, McLaren Building, 35 Dale End, Birmingham B4 7NP UK. No date.

Sastry et al. ND. Sastry R, Orlemann J, Koval P. Mercury Contamination from Metal Scrap Processing Facilities: A Study by Ohio EPA, Paper 947. No date.

USGS. 1999. U.S. Geological Survey Minerals Yearbook.

USGS. 2001. U.S. Geological Survey Minerals Yearbook.

USGS. 2002. U.S. Geological Survey Minerals Yearbook.

USGS, 2003 Cadmium Recycling in the United States in 2000.

USGS. 2006. U.S. Geological Survey Minerals Yearbook.

VADEQ. 2001. Precious Metal Recovery: Photographic Silver. Virginia Department of Environmental Quality, Waste Management. Revision 6/12/01. http://www.deq.state.va.us/waste/hazardous3.html.

Washington. 2002. Preventing Lead Poisoning in Scrap Metal Recycling, Safety & Health Assessment & Research for Prevention (SHARP), University of Washington, Seattle, WA. May 2002.

Appendix: Exposure Limits for Selected Metals

SUBSTANCE	NIOSH REL	OSHA PEL
Aluminum Metal (as Al)	10 mg/m³ (total dust) 5 mg/m³ (resp)	15 mg/m³ as Al (total) 5 mg/m³ (resp)
pyro powders and welding fumes	5 mg/m³	
soluble salts and alkyls	2 mg/m³	
Antimony and compounds except Stibine (as Sb)	0.5 mg/m³	0.5 mg/m³
Arsenic, inorganic compounds (as As);	Ca C 0.002 mg/m³ [15-minute]	0.010 mg/m³ see 1910.1018
Arsenic, organic compounds (as As)	none	0.5 mg/m³
Arsine	Ca C 0.002 mg/m³ [15-minute]	0.05 ppm (0.2 mg/m³)
Barium, soluble compounds, except Barium Sulfate (as Ba)	0.5 mg/m³	0.5 mg/m³
Barium sulfate	10 mg/m³ (total dust) 5 mg/m³ (resp)	15 mg/m³ (total) 5 mg/m³ (resp)
Beryllium and compounds (as Be)	Ca Not to exceed 0.0005 mg/m³	0.002 mg/m³ C 0.005 mg/m³ 0.025 mg/m³ [30-minute maximum peak]
Bismuth telluride, Undoped	10 mg/m³ (total) 5 mg/m³ (resp)	15 mg/m³ (total) 5 mg/m³ (resp)
Bismuth telluride, Se-doped	5 mg/m³	
Cadmium and compounds (as Cd)	Ca	0.005 mg/m³ see 1910.1027
Chromium (VI) compounds Chromic acid and chromates	(as Cr) Ca 0.001 mg/m³	(as Cr) C 0.005 mg/m³ see 1910.1026
Chromium (II) compounds (as Cr)	0.5 mg/m³	0.5 mg/m³
Chromium (III) compounds (as Cr)	0.5 mg/m³	0.5 mg/m³
Chromium metal (as Cr)	0.5 mg/m³	1 mg/m³
Chromium insoluble salts (as Cr)	0.5 mg/m³	1 mg/m³
Cobalt metal, dust, and fume (as Co)	0.05 mg/m³	0.1 mg/m³
Cobalt carbonyl	0.1 mg/m³	
Cobalt hydrocarbonyl	0.1 mg/m³	
Copper, fume (as Cu)	0.1 mg/m³	0.1 mg/m³
Copper, dust and mist (as Cu)	1 mg/m³	1 mg/m³
Hafnium and compounds (as Hf)	0.5 mg/m³	0.5 mg/m³
Hydrogen selenide (as Se)	0.05 ppm (0.2 mg/m³)	0.05 ppm (0.2 mg/m³)
Iron oxide	5 mg/m³ dust and fume	10 mg/m³ fume
Iron salts, soluble as Fe	1 mg/m³	
Lead inorganic (as Pb)	0.050 mg/m³	0.050 mg/m³ see 1910.1025
Lead Chromate	See "Lead inorganic" and "Chromic acid & chromates"	See "Lead inorganic" and "Chromic acid & chromates"
Magnesium oxide fume		15 mg/m³

SUBSTANCE	NIOSH REL	OSHA PEL
Manganese compounds (as Mn)	1 mg/m³ ST 3 mg/m³	C 5 mg/m³
Manganese fume (as Mn)	1 mg/m³ ST 3 mg/m³	C 5 mg/m³
Mercury (organo) alkyl compounds (as Hg)	0.01 mg/m³ ST 0.03 mg/m³ [skin]	0.01 mg/m³ C 0.04 mg/m³
Mercury (Elemental and Inorganic form)	C 0.1 mg/m³ [skin]	C 0.1 mg/m³
Mercury vapor	0.05 mg/m³ [skin]	C 0.1 mg/m³
Molybdenum insoluble compounds (as Mo)		15 mg/m³
Molybdenum soluble compounds		5 mg/m³
Nickel carbonyl (as Ni)	Ca 0.001 ppm (0.007 mg/m³)	0.001 ppm (0.007 mg/m³)
Nickel, metal (as Ni)	Ca 0.015 mg/m³	1 mg/m³
Nickel, insoluble compounds (as Ni)	Ca 0.015 mg/m³	1 mg/m³
Nickel, soluble compounds (as Ni)	Ca 0.015 mg/m³	1 mg/m³
Osmium tetroxide (as Os)	0.002 mg/m³ (0.0002 ppm) ST 0.006 mg/m³ (0.0006 ppm)	0.002 mg/m³
Platinum, metal	1 mg/m³	none
Platinum, soluble salts (as Pt)	0.002 mg/m³	0.002 mg/m³
Rhodium (as Rh), metal fume and insoluble compounds	0.1 mg/m³	0.1 mg/m³
Rhodium (as Rh), soluble compounds	0.001 mg/m³	0.001 mg/m³
Selenium and compounds (as Se)	0.2 mg/m³	0.2 mg/m³
Selenium hexafluoride (as Se)	0.05 ppm	0.05 ppm (0.4 mg/m³)
Silver, metal (as Ag)	0.01 mg/m³	0.01 mg/m³
Silver, soluble compounds (as Ag)	0.01 mg/m³	0.01 mg/m³
Stibine (Antimony hydride)	0.1 ppm (0.5 mg/m³)	0.1 ppm (0.5 mg/m³)
Tantalum, metal and oxide dust	5 mg/m³ ST 10 mg/m³	5 mg/m³
Tellurium and compounds (as Te)	0.1 mg/m³	0.1 mg/m³
Tellurium hexafluoride (as Te)	0.02 ppm (0.2 mg/m³)	0.02 ppm (0.2 mg/m³)
Tetraethyl lead (as Pb)	0.075 mg/m³ [skin]	0.075 mg/m³ [skin]
Tetramethyl lead (as Pb)	0.075 mg/m³ [skin]	0.075 mg/m³ [skin]
Thallium, soluble compounds (as Tl)	0.1 mg/m³ [skin]	0.1 mg/m³ [skin]
Tin, inorganic compounds (except oxides) (as Sn)	2 mg/m³	2 mg/m³
Tin, organic compounds (as Sn)	0.1 mg/m³ [skin]	0.1 mg/m³
Tin(II) oxide	2 mg/m³	
Tin(IV) oxide	2 mg/m³	
Titanium dioxide	Ca	15 mg/m³
Uranium, soluble compounds	Ca 0.05 mg/m³	0.05 mg/m³

SUBSTANCE	NIOSH REL	OSHA PEL
Uranium, insoluble compounds	Ca 0.2 mg/m³ ST 0.6 mg/m³	0.25 mg/m³
Vanadium, dust	C 0.05 mg/m³ [15-minute] (as V)	C 0.05 mg/m³ (as V2O5) (resp)
Vanadium, fumes	C 0.05 mg/m³ [15-minute] (as V)	C 0.1 mg/m³ (as V2O5)
Yttrium and compounds (as Y)	1 mg/m³	1 mg/m³
Zinc chloride fume	1 mg/m³ ST 2 mg/m³	1 mg/m³
Zinc oxide fume	5 mg/m³ ST 10 mg/m³	5 mg/m³
Zinc oxide dust	5 mg/m³ C 15 mg/m³	15 mg/m³ (total) 5 mg/m³ (resp)
Zinc stearate	10 mg/m³ (total) 5 mg/m³ (resp)	
Zirconium compounds (as Zr)	5 mg/m³ ST 10 mg/m³ (as Zr) (except Zirconium tetrachloride.)	5 mg/m³

Sources: 29 CFR 1910.1000 Table Z-1; 29 CFR 1910.1000 Table Z-2; National Institute for Occupational Safety and Health (NIOSH) Pocket Guide, Publication 97-140, February 2004.

Legend of Acronyms and Notations for Appendix A

General

mg/m³	milligrams per cubic meter		**Substances**
ppm	parts per million	A	Aluminum
resp	respirable fraction of the airborne particulate	Ag	Silver
skin	indicates the potential for dermal absorption	As	Arsenic
total	total airborne particulate	Ba	Barium
C	ceiling	Be	Beryllium
		Cd	Cadmium
		Co	Cobalt
		Cr	Chromium
		CrO₃	Chromium Oxide
		Cu	Copper
		Fe	Iron
		Hf	Hafnium
		Hg	Mercury
		Mn	Manganese
		Mo	Molybdenum

Substances (continued):

Ni	Nickel
Os	Osmium
Pb	Lead
Pb₃(AsO₄)₂	Lead Arsenate
Pt	Platinum
Rh	Rhodium
Sb	Antimony
Se	Selenium
Sn	Tin
Te	Tellurium
Tl	Thallium
V	Vanadium
V₂O₅	Vanadium Pentoxide
Y	Yttrium
Zr	Zirconium

NIOSH

Ca	carcinogen
REL	recommended exposure limit
ST	Short term exposure limit

OSHA

PEL	permissible exposure limit
skin	indicates the potential for dermal absorption

OSHA Assistance

OSHA can provide extensive help through a variety of programs, including technical assistance about effective safety and health programs, state plans, workplace consultations, voluntary protection programs, strategic partnerships, training and education, and more. An overall commitment to workplace safety and health can add value to your business, to your workplace, and to your life.

Safety and Health Program Management Guidelines

Effective management of employee safety and health protection is a decisive factor in reducing the extent and severity of work-related injuries and illnesses and their related costs. In fact, an effective safety and health program forms the basis of good employee protection and can save time and money (about $4 for every dollar spent) and increase productivity and reduce employee injuries, illnesses, and related workers' compensation costs.

To assist employers and employees in developing effective safety and health programs, OSHA published recommended Safety and Health Program Management Guidelines (54 *Federal Register* (16): 3904-3916, January 26, 1989). These voluntary guidelines can be applied to all places of employment covered by OSHA.

The guidelines identify four general elements critical to the development of a successful safety and health management system:

- Management leadership and employee involvement,
- Worksite analysis,
- Hazard prevention and control, and
- Safety and health training.

The guidelines recommend specific actions, under each of these general elements, to achieve an effective safety and health program. The Federal Register notice is available online at www.osha.gov.

State Programs

The Occupational Safety and Health Act of 1970 (OSH Act) encourages states to develop and operate their own job safety and health plans. OSHA approves and monitors these plans. Twenty-four states, Puerto Rico, and the Virgin Islands currently operate approved state plans: 22 cover both private and public (state and local government) employment; Connecticut, New Jersey, New York, and the Virgin Islands cover the public sector only. States and territories with their own OSHA-approved occupational safety and health plans must adopt standards identical to, or at least as effective as, the Federal OSHA standards.

Consultation Services

Consultation assistance is available on request to employers who want help in establishing and maintaining a safe and healthful workplace. Largely funded by OSHA, the service is provided at no cost to the employer. Primarily developed for smaller employers with more hazardous operations, the consultation service is delivered by state governments employing professional safety and health consultants. Comprehensive assistance includes an appraisal of all mechanical systems, work practices, and occupational safety and health hazards of the workplace and all aspects of the employer's present job safety and health program. In addition, the service offers assistance to employers in developing and implementing an effective safety and health program. No penalties are proposed or citations issued for hazards identified by the consultant. OSHA provides consultation assistance to the employer with the assurance that his or her name and firm and any information about the workplace will not be routinely reported to OSHA enforcement staff.

Under the consultation program, certain exemplary employers may request participation in OSHA's Safety and Health Achievement Recognition Program (SHARP). Eligibility for participation in SHARP includes receiving a comprehensive consultation visit, demonstrating exemplary achievements in workplace safety and health by abating all identified hazards, and developing an excellent safety and health program.

Employers accepted into SHARP may receive an exemption from programmed inspections (not complaint or accident investigation inspections) for a period of 1 year. For more information concerning consultation assistance, see OSHA's website at www.osha.gov.

Voluntary Protection Programs (VPP)

Voluntary Protection Programs and on-site consultation services, when coupled with an effective enforcement program, expand employee protection to help meet the goals of the OSH Act. The VPPs motivate others to achieve excellent safety and health results in the same outstanding way as they establish a cooperative relationship between employers, employees, and OSHA.

For additional information on VPP and how to apply, contact the OSHA regional offices listed at the end of this publication.

Strategic Partnership Program

OSHA's Strategic Partnership Program, the newest member of OSHA's cooperative programs, helps encourage, assist, and recognize the efforts of partners to eliminate serious workplace hazards and achieve a high level of employee safety and health. Whereas OSHA's Consultation Program and VPP entail one-on-one relationships between OSHA and individual worksites, most strategic partnerships seek to have a broader impact by building cooperative relationships with groups of employers and employees. These partnerships are voluntary, cooperative relationships between OSHA, employers, employee representatives, and others (e.g., trade unions, trade and professional associations, universities, and other government agencies).

For more information on this and other cooperative programs, contact your nearest OSHA office, or visit OSHA's website at www.osha.gov.

Alliance Program

Through the Alliance Program, OSHA works with groups committed to safety and health, including businesses, trade or professional organizations, unions and educational institutions, to leverage resources and expertise to develop compliance assistance tools and resources and share information with employers and employees to help prevent injuries, illnesses and fatalities in the workplace.

Alliance program agreements have been established with a wide variety of industries including meat, apparel, poultry, steel, plastics, maritime, printing, chemical, construction, paper and telecommunications. These agreements are addressing many safety and health hazards and at-risk audiences, including silica, fall protection, amputations, immigrant workers, youth and small businesses. By meeting the goals of the Alliance Program agreements (training and education, outreach and communication, and promoting the national dialogue on workplace safety and health), OSHA and the Alliance Program participants are developing and disseminating compliance assistance information and resources for employers and employees such as electronic assistance tools, fact sheets, toolbox talks, and training programs.

OSHA Training and Education

OSHA area offices offer a variety of information services, such as compliance assistance, technical advice, publications, audiovisual aids, and speakers for special engagements. OSHA's Training Institute in Arlington Heights, IL, provides basic and advanced courses in safety and health for Federal and state compliance officers, state consultants, Federal agency personnel, and private sector employers, employees, and their representatives.

The OSHA Training Institute also has established OSHA Training Institute Education Centers to address the increased demand for its courses from the private sector and from other federal agencies. These centers include colleges, universities, and nonprofit training organizations that have been selected after a competition for participation in the program.

OSHA also provides funds to nonprofit organizations, through grants, to conduct workplace training and education in subjects where OSHA believes there is a lack of workplace training. Grants are awarded annually. Grant recipients are expected to contribute 20 percent of the total grant cost.

For more information on training and education, contact the OSHA Training Institute, Directorate of Training and Education, 2020 South Arlington Heights Road, Arlington Heights, IL, 60005, (847) 297-4810, or see Training on OSHA's website at www.osha.gov. For further information on any OSHA program, contact your nearest OSHA regional office listed at the end of this publication.

Information Available Electronically

OSHA has a variety of materials and tools available on its website at www.osha.gov. These include electronic compliance assistance tools, such as *Safety and Health Topics Pages, eTools, Expert Advisors;* regulations, directives, publications and videos; and other information for employers and employees. OSHA's software programs and compliance assistance tools walk you through challenging safety and health issues and common problems to find the best solutions for your workplace.

A wide variety of OSHA materials, including standards, interpretations, directives, and more can be purchased on CD-ROM from the U.S. Government Printing Office, Superintendent of Documents, toll-free phone (866) 512-1800.

Occupational Safety and Health Administration

OSHA Publications

OSHA has an extensive publications program. For a listing of free or sales items, visit OSHA's website at www.osha.gov or contact the OSHA Publications Office, U.S. Department of Labor, 200 Constitution Avenue, NW, N-3101, Washington, DC 20210: Telephone (202) 693-1888 or fax to (202) 693-2498.

Contacting OSHA

To report an emergency, file a complaint, or seek OSHA advice, assistance, or products, call (800) 321-OSHA or contact your nearest OSHA Regional office listed at the end of this publication. The teletypewriter (TTY) number is (877) 889-5627.

Written correspondence can be mailed to the nearest OSHA Regional or Area Office listed at the end of this publication or to OSHA's national office at: U.S. Department of Labor, Occupational Safety and Health Administration, 200 Constitution Avenue, N.W., Washington, DC 20210.

By visiting OSHA's website at www.osha.gov, you can also:

- File a complaint online,
- Submit general inquiries about workplace safety and health electronically, and
- Find more information about OSHA and occupational safety and health.

OSHA Regional Offices

Region I
(CT,* ME, MA, NH, RI, VT*)
JFK Federal Building, Room E340
Boston, MA 02203
(617) 565-9860

Region II
(NJ,* NY,* PR,* VI*)
201 Varick Street, Room 670
New York, NY 10014
(212) 337-2378

Region III
(DE, DC, MD,* PA, VA,* WV)
The Curtis Center
170 S. Independence Mall West
Suite 740 West
Philadelphia, PA 19106-3309
(215) 861-4900

Region IV
(AL, FL, GA, KY,* MS, NC,* SC,* TN*)
61 Forsyth Street, SW, Room 6T50
Atlanta, GA 30303
(404) 562-2300

Region V
(IL, IN,* MI,* MN,* OH, WI)
230 South Dearborn Street
Room 3244
Chicago, IL 60604
(312) 353-2220

Region VI
(AR, LA, NM,* OK, TX)
525 Griffin Street, Room 602
Dallas, TX 75202
(972) 850-4145

Region VII
(IA,* KS, MO, NE)
Two Pershing Square
2300 Main Street, Suite 1010
Kansas City, MO 64108-2416
(816) 283-8745

Region VIII
(CO, MT, NO, SO, UT,* WY*)
1999 Broadway, Suite 1690
PO Box 46550
Denver, CO 80202-5716
(720) 264-6550

Region IX
(American Samoa, AZ,* CA,* HI,* NV,* GM,
Northern Mariana Islands)
90 7th Street, Suite 18-100
San Francisco, CA 94103
(415) 625-2547

Region X
(AK,* ID, OR,* WA*)
1111 Third Avenue, Suite 715
Seattle, WA 98101-3212
(206) 553-5930

* These states and territories operate their own OSHA-approved job safety and health programs and cover state and local government employees as well as private sector employees. The Connecticut, New Jersey, New York and Virgin Islands plans cover public employees only. States with approved programs must have standards that are identical to, or at least as effective as, the Federal standards.

Note: To get contact information for OSHA Area Offices, OSHA-approved State Plans and OSHA Consultation Projects, please visit us online at www.osha.gov or call us at 1-800-321-0SHA.

www.ingramcontent.com/pod-product-compliance
Lightning Source LLC
Chambersburg PA
CBHW081753170526

45167CB00009B/4014